Antiqu

Guide to

Fake & Forged Marks

L. C. Tiffany - Favrile

Mark Chervenka

Published by

 **krause
publications**

700 E. State Street • Iola, WI 54990-0001
Telephone: 715/445-2214
Web: www.krause.com

Please call or write for our free catalog of publications.
Our toll-free number to place an order or obtain a free catalog is 800-258-0929
or please use our regular business telephone 715-445-2214.

Library of Congress Catalog Number: 2002105085
ISBN: 0-87349-436-9

Printed in the United States of America

Contents

Tools to catch fakes and reproductions

6" black light

Take anywhere in your pocket or purse; 4 watt long- wave, 6 month warranty on circuitry, 30 day warranty on bulb. Uses 4AA batteries (not included)

$24.00+ $3 shipping

mini black light

A pocket powerhouse that flouresces vaseline glass and many other materials in room lighting. Use for bone, ivory, glue, invisible inks and most credit cards and currency. 2¾-inch virtually crushproof metal case; true longwave, includes key loop and snap swivel, includes removable30-inch all weather neck loop, SIX FREE BATTERIES

$12.50 each + shpg
two for $21.50 FREE shpg

Black Light Book

Enlarged 4th edition. Complete tests for fakes, reproductions, damages and repairs; 112 pgs; 109 illus. 6x9-inches, softcover. China, pottery, ivory, paper, textiles, gemstones, glass, paintings, prints, etc. How to use invisible inks for secret marks, to prevent returns, readmission, etc.

$14.95+ $2.50 shipping
($9.95 +shpg with any black light)

Diamond loupe 10X color corrected, distortion free triplet glass lens 5/8-inch dia. Leather case and hanging loop. Compare at $30-$45.
#AC-$19.95 + $2.75 shipping

satisfaction guaranteed–same day shipping

Antique & Collectors Reproduction News
PO Box 12130   Des Moines, Iowa 50312   1-515-274-5886 M
www.repronews.com

How to Use This Book

This is not just another book of marks.

Marks in this book include fakes and reproductions. Rather than a straight alphabetical list of marks, the marks are arranged by subject or the material to which they are applied. Marks then are listed alphabetically within the respective chapters. Where possible, I've tried to show both the fake and original markings side by side.

You'll find many entries simply include the mark and a brief explanation and date. Others–such as Thomas Webb, Rookwood, Wedgwood and similar companies with long and involved histories–include more detailed explanations. Some subjects which collectors have found particularly confusing, such as Royal Dux, or have become the special target of widespread forgeries, such as blue transfer ware, have their own chapters.

The index is very detailed and you should begin your search there. Indexed entries are arranged alphabetically by the main or dominant word in the mark. Although the index follows traditional styles, there are some exceptions. For example, names of marks that contain a personal name are listed by the first letter that appears in the mark, not necessarily the last name. CH Haviland, for example, is indexed under C, not Haviland. J. Finkelstein and Son, is entered under J. You can also search the index for specific categories based on material such as Majolica, and by some shapes, such as cookie jars.

The only real mistake you can make with this book is to think it contains all the marks being faked and forged. Far from it. New marks are discovered every day. And just because you don't find a mark here, doesn't mean it isn't being reproduced.

Mark J. Chervenka
Editor/publisher
Antique & Collectors Reproduction News
The monthly newsletter on fakes and reproductions since 1992

Art Glass

New piece of iridescent art glass. The original engraved maker's mark (shown opposite page) is easily removed and replaced with a forged mark.

Due to its high value, art glass is a frequent target of reproductions, especially fake and forged marks and signatures.

Fake marks are now so common they should never be used as a single test of age or authenticity. It has become more important than ever to know and understand what original marks are appropriate for the pieces to which they are applied and how original marks and signatures were made. In other words, learn which marks were used during what years and which should be acid-etched, which wheel-engraved, and which appear only as paper labels.

Most forgers use modern tools that make their work quick and easy, but not necessarily historically accurate. That's why you'll see marks originally appearing only as paper labels show up as acid-etched forgeries, or vice versa.

The vast majority of authentic marks on iridescent art glass like

Original dated 1992 mark that appears on the pontil of the new iridescent studio glass shown on the opposite page.

New dated mark is ground out at a glass repair shop. It's now ready for a forged mark of some vintage maker such as Steuben, Tiffany, Loetz or others.

Forged "Loetz" mark engraved on pontil where modern name and date was removed.

Close up of new mark engraved with electric pen. Note characteristic skips in curve (arrow).

Art Glass

A new "pontil" mark applied by sandblasting, then polishing. This mark was applied to a modern molded piece of glass which was altered to resemble a piece of old blown glass.

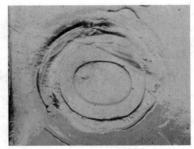

Tiffany, Steuben and Loetz, for example, were engraved with rotating ball-shaped burrs or the very edges of wheels. Engraved numbers and letters have a ragged-edged, shaky or jerky look (shown in the following pages). This is because only the very edge of the wheel made contact with the glass. Wheel-engraved authentic marks usually have a frosted, dull appearance, although this will vary somewhat from manufacturer to manufacturer.

Modern forgeries of engraved marks are most commonly made with carbide bits or diamond-tipped tools, not wheels. These modern tool bits typically produce a continuous flowing line with a smooth, clean edge (see the following pages). Diamond and carbide tips actually cut–rather than grind–the glass.

Original wheel-engraved marks are generally, but not always, much smaller than forged marks. It's as though forgers don't want to take a chance you might miss the mark. Numbers and letters in original engraved marks of Tiffany and Lalique, for example, are rarely taller than one-quarter inch; most are one-eighth to three-sixteenths inch. Marks purported to be from any vintage maker with letters larger than one-half inch all should be viewed with extreme suspicion.

Since engraved marks were hand applied, there is considerable variation in appearance among original marks in size, legibility, and style. There is no single "right" engraved mark for any of the original companies. There is no set or standard location where original marks appear. Many authentic marks, particularly Tiffany and Steuben, run around the edge of the pontil but can appear in other areas as well.

There are many other forged marks besides the ones shown in the following pages. Remember, never use marks alone as a test of age. Marks are widely forged on both new glass and on old but originally unmarked glass by less well known makers. Many pieces of genuinely old unmarked Czech glass from the 1930s, for example, frequently turn up with forged Lalique marks.

Tools used to forge marks on glass

Edges of small wheels were used to engrave marks on most authentic
19th and early 20th century art glass.

Any black and white artwork can be converted into a new rubber stamp. These
stamps are widely used by forgers to apply fake acid marks. Most new stamped
acid marks are blurred and uneven.

 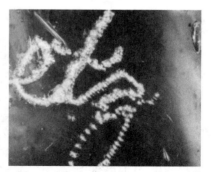

Electric pens have bits that vibrate from side to side that produce a line with
skips and gaps and a "shaky" appearance.

Art Glass

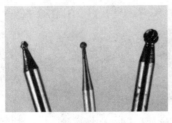

Modern carbide grinding bits leave smooth-edged canal-like marks.

Industrial diamond-tipped pencils produce very thin scratch-like lines.

Amberina

Amberina is an American art glass shading from amber to red. It was developed by Joseph Locke and first made by New England Glass Co. in 1883 and remained in production until about 1888. The original 19th century amberina was marked only with a paper label, very few of which have survived.

In 1888, the New England Glass Co. changed its name to the Libbey Glass Co. and moved to Toledo, Ohio. Libbey attempted to reintroduce a slightly different form of amberina in 1917. Libbey's ca. 1917 amberina shades to a distinctive fuchsia rather than cranberry red. The new amberina was not successful and made for only a limited time.

Many, but not all, pieces of Libbey amberina are marked with an acid stamp. There are two versions. One has the word "amberina" spelled out with the word "Libbey" below in script enclosed in a circle. The combination Amberina/Libbey mark is slightly over one-half inch wide.

No authentic New England Glass Co. or Libbey Glass Co. amberina was ever marked in any other way. Any engraved mark that includes "amberina" or "Libbey amberina" is a fake.

Genuine The only amberina permanently marked is Libbey amberina, made in 1917. Many, but far from all, Libbey amberina is marked with an acid stamp. There are two authentic versions, one with Amberina spelled out, left, and another with Libbey enclosed in a circle, right.

Baccarat

During the 1970s, Venetian glass workers made many items including paperweights, for American wholesalers of antique reproductions. A number of new paperweights included 19th century dates in imitation of famous antique paperweight maker Baccarat.

New dates in the Italian reproductions almost always appear on a single cane. That is to say, the four numbers composing the year all appear on the surface of one relatively large cane. The new single "dated" cane is generally the same diameter and thickness as decora-

Genuine Authentic year date on four separate canes. Note small size of date canes to decorative cane on left.

New date years generally appear on a single cane about the same size as all the other canes in the paperweight.

Original Baccarat paperweight with date numbers made from individual canes.

New paperweight "dated" 1852 on one large cane. Single date cane same size as decorative canes.

Art Glass

tive canes within the same weight.

Although well known for its famous paperweights, Baccarat's main production has been and continues to be fine cut crystal. The most common authentic mark on clear cut crystal is a circular design that may appear as either an acid stamp or a paper label. There are numerous fake acid stamps, the most common is simply the word "Baccarat" in a straight line (see example below). Most attempts to fake the circular mark result in smudged and blurred letters. Authentic circular acid stamps are quite small, just slightly over one-quarter inch diameter with sharp lettering (also see Baccarat in the Cameo Glass section).

Authentic Baccarat mark found as acid stamp or paper label.

Baccarat

Forgery Common acid etched forgeries appear as a straight line of block letters.

Barolac

A line of frosted glass made by the Czech firm of Joseph Inwald, ca. 1920-1939. Some original pieces are opalescent, as well as frosted. If marked, pieces usually have Barolac in molded cursive lettering. Other pieces are simply marked Czechoslovakia in molded block letters.

There is some confusion about the relationship between Barolac and the British merchant John Jenkins. Inwald glass will sometimes be found with paper labels having both Barolac and Jenkins' names. Some authors have interpreted these labels to mean that Barolac was

Molded mark of Barolac glass. This mark should never appear as and acid stamp.

Group of original Inwald catalogs. Note the Barolac catalog (arrow) in back. *Courtesy Robert and Deborah Truitt.*

a trade name of Jenkins, but that is not correct. At this time, it appears that Jenkins was simply an importer of Barolac glass.

Burmese

See under "Webb-Queens Burmese" in this chapter.

Crown Milano

A line of art glass made by Mt. Washington Glass Co., ca. 1893. A handpainted monogram of a C and M under crown in blue or bluish-purple paint. A four-digit design or shape number usually, but not always, appears near the mark. Original marks were applied with paintbrushes and typically show thin and thick strokes. Usually some parts of typical old marks, often the tips of the crown, are raised.

Fakes are commonly rubber stamped, leaving a mark perfectly flat rather than raised and often smeared or smudged. If a seller is offering two or more pieces with identical appearing marks, there is a good chance the mark is rubber stamped. Original marks were individually painted and no two marks are identical. Original marks are permanent. Most fakes come off with fingernail polish remover (acetone).

Genuine Two original Crown Milano marks. Authentic marks show wide variations because they are individually painted. Many forgeries are simply rubber stamped in various colors of ink.

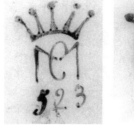

Dorflinger & Sons

Colored and cut glass, ca. 1865-1921. This trademark was used as a paper label only; it was never acid etched or engraved.

Genuine Dorflinger trademark was never used as a mark directly on glass. Used as a paper label only.

Fake Typical acid-etched forgeries like this one are usually blurred with filled-in letters and filled-in crosshatching on the decanter.

Art Glass

Czechoslovakia

See listings in this chapter under Loetz, Kralik, Barolac and Tchécoslovaquie.

Durand

Victor Durand owned a large industrial glass works, Vineland Flint Glass Works, which made industrial products such as tubing, light bulbs and laboratory glass. In 1924, he hired former Quezal employee Martin Bach Jr. to start Durand Art Glass for the production of decorative glassware.

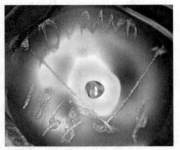

Bach's father was cofounder of Quezal Art Glass Co. and Martin Jr. brought many of his father's formulas to Durand. Durand art wares were only made from 1924 to 1931. Few pieces of original Durand are marked. Authentic marks were applied by hand with an aluminum pencil, which leaves a silvery mark. The three basic original Durand

Typical authentic Duran signature within polished pontil.

marks are shown below and on the following page. Each is in a ground pontil to show the relative size of each mark. Model, catalog and shape numbers often appear with the basic mark.

Letters in the top two basic marks often have a disjointed appearance. Letters in those marks do not always connect perfectly letter-to-letter. The third original mark is much smaller than other marks and appears the most like a handwritten single word, rather than a disjointed, loose collection of individual letters.

Genuine The word DURAND, all upper case and hand written, placed inside a large letter V. Entire mark fits inside the ground pontil.

Genuine The word DURAND handwritten in uppercase letters. Although larger than the first mark, it also fits within the ground pontil.

Genuine Handwritten Durand with capital D and lower case following letters. Significantly smaller than other marks.

Forged acid-etched "Durand" mark. No acid marks were ever used by Durand.

Eisch Glass

Contemporary glass maker in Germany which makes new studio glass, many pieces in Art Nouveau designs. This piece is dated 2001, but many pieces are without a date.

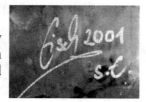

Fry Glass Co.

Makers of cut glass and art glass, ca. 1901-1933.

Genuine small acid-etched script mark, about three-sixteenths of an inch tall.

Genuine script in shield, under three-eighths inch tall.

Forged acid-etched script mark with large fat letters, over one-quarter inch tall. Often smudged with ragged edged appearance.

FRY Co.

Forged acid-etched block-letter fantasy mark. No old counterpart.

Rockwell Silver Co. estab. 1905. Applied sterling trim to Fry and other art glass. Authentic mark is an acid etched shield mark.

Genuine acid-etched mark.

Fry Rockwell Co. **Fantasy** acid-etched script mark.

Art Glass

Harrach

Bohemian glass works founded ca. 1714, still in operation today. Research by Robert and Deborah Truitt have positively traced this so-called propeller mark to Harrach family coat of arms. Painted or stamped, usually black occasionally red (also see Thomas Webb in this chapter).

Honesdale Decorating Co., ca. 1901-1932

Also see main entry in Cut Glass chapter.

Genuine Script mark appears in gold only. Any acid-etched or engraved marks are fakes.

Paper label only This monogram, made of the letters H, D and C intertwined with a goblet, was used on paper labels only. Any other use is a forgery.

Kralik

Wilhem Kralik Söhne was an important glass works in the Austria-Bohemia region of eastern Europe. It was founded in 1815 and made high quality art glass through 1933.

Although the name Kralik does not appear on glass, a very distinctive form of "Czechoslovakia" is attributed to Kralik on glass it made, ca. 1919-1933. This mark appears as an arched acid stamp. Note that the two letter Os are split down the center. Robert and Deborah Truitt, Bohemian glass experts, estimate 60 to 70 percent of pieces with this mark are Kralik products.

Two examples of arched acid-etched marks attributed to Wilhem Kralik Söhne, ca. 1919-1933. This is one of the few Czechoslovakia acid stamps on glass that can be attributed to a specific maker.

Lalique

There are several considerations when evaluating Lalique. There are genuine Lalique pieces made after 1945 with forged pre-1945 marks; new glass (especially frosted glass) with forged Lalique marks and pre-1945 glass by other manufacturers with forged Lalique marks.

Generally, all authentic Lalique glass, whether made before 1945 or after 1945, is marked. Words contained in the mark largely depends on how the mark was created. Molded marks before 1945 in *pressed* glass items were generally R LALIQUE in all uppercase, sans-serif (block style) lettering. One exception is the so-called "long L" mark (see illustrations). It never appeared with the letter R.

The great majority of authentic Lalique molded marks from before and after 1945 appear as raised lettering. Some authentic molded marks are in intaglio–below the surface–but most molded marks are raised. The word France may or may not be included in authentic molded marks. If France is included in a molded mark, it may appear on the same line as R Lalique or on a separate line. The R was removed from virtually all molded marks after 1945.

Before 1945, engraved marks were applied primarily to *mold-blown* glass. If molded marks were faint, an engraved mark might be added, producing a piece having two marks. Mold-blown pieces usually can be identified by a ground and polished pontil in the base of the piece. Pressed glass pieces, by contrast, commonly have ground bottom rims but not ground pontils.

Most engraved marks before 1926 were simply R Lalique applied with a rotating engraving burr. While these original marks show considerable variation in size, exact nature and form, they still maintain a certain continuity. The R in particular is engraved with the same general style from mark to mark.

France may or may not appear in authentic pre-1945 engraved marks. As a general rule, France appears more often in engraved marks after 1926, the year England required the country of origin to be permanently applied to all imported goods.

Since 1980, Lalique engraved marks have also included the modern ® symbol, an R in a circle. The only marks referring to registration on pre-1945 marks generally appear as Reg or Reg'd meaning the design was filed within the British registry system for protection. The single letter R is commonly forged on post-1945 Lalique engraved marks to suggest a piece was made before 1945.

Lalique original molded marks

R. LALIQUE

Pre-1945 molded Authentic molded marks are sans-serif, block style letters. France may or may not be included. Authentic molded marks appear primarily in pressed glass.

Pre-1945 molded Almost all molded marks in pressed glass appear as raised letters above the surface. Shown as line drawing above, photo below. Note block-style letters.

View from back

Pre-1945 molded Some marks are molded in reverse. The raised glass letters in this example are molded on the bottom of a plate. Looking at the letters from the bottom, they appear reversed. Looking through the front side, the letters appear correctly.

Front view looking through glass.

Pre-1945 molded Some molded marks have a double-tailed Q. Marks with double-tailed Qs, like other molded marks, appear as raised lettering. The mark can appear within the pattern, or around top and bottom rims. France may or may not appear.

Typical molded marks with double-tailed Q.

Pre-1945 molded This is one of the exceptions to the general rule that pre-1945 authentic marks should include an R. This authentic molded mark, the so-called "long L," never appeared with an R. This molded mark was used far less often than the standard block letter molded mark. It is most commonly seen on perfume bottles and dresser items.

Raised "long-L" molded mark did not include either France or the letter R.

Lalique–original engraved marks

Pre-1945 engraved Genuine engraved R. Lalique France. Engraved marks were usually applied to mold-blown, not pressed pieces. Although there is considerable variation among genuine engraved marks, almost all have the same general appearance as the examples shown on this page. Note in particular the way the R is formed in all the examples.

Pre-1945 engraved Genuine engraved R. Lalique France. May include an order, catalog or merchant number. The presence or absence of a number is not a test of age or authenticity.

Pre-1945 engraved Genuine engraved R. Lalique France. Most, but not all, engraved marks were applied to mold-blown pieces. Pressed pieces generally were marked in the mold. However, if the molded mark was weak, an engraved signature might be added.

Pre-1945 engraved Genuine engraved marks may appear in a single line or two lines.

Post-1945 engraved The letter R, for Rene, has not been included in authentic engraved marks since 1945. Since 1980, Lalique marks have also included the modern registration symbol, an R in a circle, ®.

Wheel-cut marks were made with only the edges of small grinding wheels. Genuine wheel-cut marks can be identified by letters formed with a series of short straight lines usually meeting in right angles. The absence of curves gives wheel-cut letters a distinctive stiff, box-like appearance. Wheel-cut marks were first used in the 1930s.

Authentic pre-1945 Lalique etched marks were all made with sandblasting which produced frosted block letters. Genuine marks can be identified by small regular gaps in letters produced by straps that held stencils together (see illustrations). Most, but far from all, genuine etched marks include the word France.

Etched marks continued to be applied to genuine Lalique after 1945. Post-1945 marks appear without the R in front of Lalique. Whether made before 1945 or after 1945, all genuine etched marks are applied with the stencil and should show the characteristic gaps in the lettering.

Beginning in the early to mid-1950s, Lalique began using a second type of etched mark, one produced with acid. The acid marks continued the Lalique tradition of simple block-styled lettering. Genuine acid marks can be identified by their smooth uniform frosting, lack of pitting and generally very sharp edged lettering. The most common form of the acid etched mark is a single line in uppercase block letters, LALIQUE FRANCE (see illustrations).

Etched marks of both kinds, sandblasted and acid etched, have been used on post-1945 commercial perfume bottles. The best way to authenticate Lalique-made perfume bottles is by referring to a specialized list, book or catalog which describes the marks that appear on the bottles of various perfume manufacturers.

Pre-1945 clear Lalique fluoresces a soft yellow-green to yellow under long-wave black light. Clear Lalique made after 1945 does not fluoresce. If the initial "R" appeared with that symbol, it would automatically be a forgery.

Lalique original cut and etched marks

Pre-1945 wheel-cut Wheel-cut marks were made with the edge of a small grinding wheel. Letters made with grinding wheels appear as short straight lines as seen in this typical example. Wheel-cut marks were first used in the 1930s.

R. L A L I Q U E   F R A N C E

Pre-1945 etched Genuine R. Lalique France etched marks were made by sandblasting through a stencil. Genuine marks are characterized by uniform gaps in letters left by stencil straps. Genuine marks have a frosted appearance. Pre-1945 etched marks usually, but not always, include the word France.

Art Glass

Post-1945 etched Genuine etched mark without the R in front of Lalique. Note the gaps in letters left by stencil.

Pre-1945 etched Genuine R. Lalique France etched through a stencil. Note the gaps in letters left by stencil.

Pre-1945 etched Genuine R. Lalique etched through a stencil. Note the gaps in letters left by stencil.

Genuine post-1945 acid-etched mark Commercial perfume for Nina Ricci. Marked in acid-etched letters, NINA RICCI FRANCE–BOTTLE MADE BY LALIQUE.

Genuine post-1945 acid-etched mark Acid-etched marks are all uppercase block letters. No gaps in letters; fairly sharp-edged well defined letters.

Clues and warning signs of
fake and forged Lalique marks

Any of the features shown below are warning signs of a forgery. Also be suspicious of large marks placed in obvious locations such as around the neck or sides. Forgeries can be acid-etched, sandblasted, molded or engraved.

Words and phrases not associated with genuine marks

There are certain words and phrases that appear in many false marks that virtually never appeared in any authentic Lalique mark on general production pieces made either before or after 1945. Any of the following words or phrases are indications that you are most likely looking at a forged or faked mark.

Paris France

Some perfume bottles include Paris, but general production pieces do not. As a general rule, be suspicious of any marks with Paris France.

Rene Lalique

Standard marks on general production pieces before 1945 generally include only the initial R; Rene is not usually spelled out.

Made in France

Authentic Lalique marks used before 1945 and the great majority of marks used after 1945 include France only. As a general rule, any mark with Made in France is probably not genuine. Made in France does appear on a number of present-day Lalique look-alike pieces like the Art Deco frosted lamp shown here. Made in France is molded on the bottom. Many of these new pieces frequently include a forged engraved Lalique mark.

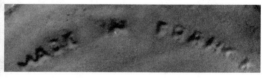

no 125/300   *#97 of 150*

Numbers which appear in authentic marks on pre-1945 Lalique are design, registry or production numbers. Any number(s) that appear as edition numbers were not used in authentic marks on Lalique made before 1945.

Style and size of lettering in marks

Except for genuine engraved markings, which are in script and uppercase and lowercase letters, all other authentic Lalique marks generally appear as uppercase block-styled, or sans-serif, letters. Serifs refer to the thin edges of letters or flourishes that extend from the body of the letter. Type styles in many forgeries are very elaborate and fanciful. Size can be another clue to authenticity. The vast majority of authentic marks before and after 1945, particularly molded, sand-blasted and acid etched, are quite small, very rarely over three-sixteenths inch in height. Engraved marks vary considerably in size, but are generally about one-quarter inch high which fits on most rims.

Warning signs

R line thickness varies from thick to thin

↑ serif

Authentic

R lines the same thickness, no serifs (sans-serif)

R Lalique

Upper and lower case.

R LALIQUE

All upper case.

Rene Lalique

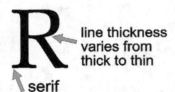

Many forgeries are one-quarter inch and larger.

R LALIQUE
LALIQUE FRANCE
R.LALIQUE

Authentic marks are rarely over one-quarter inch tall.

Location of marks

Original marks, whether engraved, molded, etched or sand-blasted, are generally placed in inconspicuous locations such as bottom rims, pontil marks or worked into the design. Many forgeries are prominently placed as if to emphasize "this piece is marked Lalique."

Appearance of etched letters

Acid-stamped post-1945 marks are among the most commonly forged Lalique marks. Authentic acid-etched marks have crisp sharp edges. The entire letter is evenly filled with smooth and continuous etched surface. Forgeries are typically smudged, not entirely filled in and areas that should be open are frequently filled in.

Typical forged marks

Here are some typical forgeries which illustrate the basic points to examine when evaluating marks on Lalique.

Clues to a typical forged acid mark

Etching appears   Normally open   Etching extends
as an outline   areas filled in   beyond edges

Engraved forgery, "Rene Lalique–France Reg #478."
Very few authentic marks have the word Rene spelled
out. In the great majority of authentic pre-1945 marks,
Rene is abbreviated as the initial R.

Art Glass

Acid-etched forgery, "R. Lalique FRANCE." No authentic pre-1945 Lalique mark was acid-etched. Authentic post-1945 acid-etched Lalique marks are all uppercase sans-serif style, not cursive and not a mixture of upper and lowercase letters.

Typical acid-etched forgery, "R. LALIQUE FRANCE." Note poorly formed letters: bottom of L touches bottom of A. Many letters appear as outlines only.

Acid-etched forgery, "R. LALIQUE FRANCE." Very streaked appearance; France is barely legible.

New frosted glass reproductions like the inexpensive perfume bottle made in Taiwan, left, are frequently seen with forged Lalique marks. Original Deaux Fleurs Lalique perfume marked R. Lalique, right.

Raised glass letter forgery, "R. LALIQUE," on the foot of a vase. Letters almost one-half inch tall. Prominent position and size totally unlike original marks.

Forged mark in intaglio, or below, the surface. Many letters touching, strong outlines with poorly filled in bodies.

Forged mark in intaglio, or below, the surface. Strange type style, strong outlines with poorly filled in bodies. Letters set on unusual curved line.

Forgery in raised glass letters made by cutting away the surrounding surface. Letters are almost one-half inch high. Original molded marks are virtually never more than one-quarter inch high, usually only about one-eighth to three-sixteenths inch tall.

Raised glass lettering forgery, "R. LALIQUE FRANCE." This elaborate type style was never used in authentic R. Lalique marks. In authentic marks, both Lalique and France are in the same type style, not two different type styles. The size of France can vary, but France virtually always appears in the same style of type as Lalique.

Engraved forgery in diamond-tip pen, "R Lalique-France." Virtually all pre-1945 authentic marks were applied with a rotating burr, not a diamond-tipped stylus. This forgered mark appears on the new bowl and underplate, below, made in Czech Republic.

Current authentic Lalique diamond-tip engraved mark, Lalique France. The mark includes the modern registry symbol, ®, an R inside a circle.

Libbey Glass

Although Libbey is best known for its cut glass, it also made several types of art glass. One of these is amberina introduced in 1917 and discussed earlier in this section. The other major group of Libbey art glass was designed by A. Douglas Nash and introduced in 1933. This group, called the Libbey-Nash series, was a financial disaster and very little was produced. Most, but far from all, of the Libbey-Nash series are marked with an acid stamp with Libbey in a circle. The Libbey in circle was never diamond engraved and was never over one-half inch in size. This circular mark never appeared on heavy brilliant period cut glass Libbey made ca. 1890-1915 (see Libbey cut glass marks in the Cut Glass chapter).

Most, but not all, authentic ca. 1932-34 Libbey-Nash pieces were usually stamped in acid with the single word Libbey in a circle. This mark is very small, typically about one-quarter inch. This mark was not used on brilliant period Libbey cut glass, ca. 1890-1915.

Another acid stamp mark on authentic Libbey-Nash pieces, ca. 1932-34 but rarely found. Also found as paper label.

Although this mark reads "Libbey Cut Glass," it was never used as a permanent mark on cut glass. It was used on cut glass only as a now rare paper label. The most common use of this mark is a red ink stamp on opaque white glass, primarily souvenirs Libbey sold at its on-site factory at the Columbian Exposition, 1892-1893. Actual size is slightly less than one-half inch diameter. See entry for Libbey in Cut Glass section for more information.

Art Glass

Loetz

Johann Lötz never owned a glass business. The iridescent glass known by his name was made at a glass factory started by his widow, Susanna, in 1851. She named the business "Johann Lötz Witwe" (the widow of Johann Lötz). The business began making common objects but turned to art glass in 1879 when Johann's grandson Maximilian Von Spaun II took control of the business. Around the turn of the 19th century, spelling of the business name was changed from Lötz to Loetz. Pieces made for export, if marked, usually read "Loetz, Austria."

Far more iridescent Loetz was originally unmarked than iridescent glass made by Tiffany or Steuben. Before Loetz prices began rising in the 1990s, many original pieces of Loetz had forged signatures of other more valuable makers like Tiffany. Now that Loetz has risen to the same price as other makers, many variations of forged Loetz marks are in the market.

First, no original Loetz mark with the word Loetz or Lötz was acid stamped. Any acid stamped mark with the word Loetz or Lötz is a forgery. All original engraved marks with Loetz or Lötz are wheel engraved. Any mark engraved with a diamond-tip pen or electric pen is a forgery. Virtually all original Loetz has fire-polished rims and ground pontils.

Between the wars, ca. 1919-1939, some grades of glass made

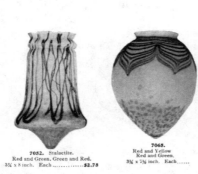

7052. Stalactite.
Red and Green, Green and Red.
3¼ x 8 inch. Each $2.75

7065.
Red and Yellow
Red and Green.
3¼ x 7½ inch. Each......

Loetz produced substantial amounts of glass shades similar to these examples for export. Lighting products are rarely marked, since they were usually sold under the importers' or wholesalers' names.

Original Loetz art glass vase, swirls in oil-spot iridescent surface.

by Loetz were marked Czechoslovakia in acid stamped letters. Two marks in particular—Czechoslovakia in an oval and Czechoslovakia in a rectangular box—have about a 90-percent probability of being Loetz, according to Robert and Deborah Truitt. Keep in mind, however, that neither Loetz or Lötz ever appeared in an acid stamped mark, only the word Czechoslovakia.

Authentic Loetz marks

Lötz
with arrows in circle
engraved.

Spaun
(nephew of Lotz)
engraved.

Joh. Lotz WWE
Klostermuehle
paper label.

Loetz, Austria All original engraved Loetz marks are wheel engraved.

Original acid-etched marks, ca. 1919-1939, attributed to Loetz. Czechoslovakia in an oval, left, and Czechoslovakia in a rectangular box, right. Neither Loetz nor Lötz ever appears in these acid-stamped marks.

Art Glass

Line drawings of authentic acid-stamped marks attributed to Loetz, ca. 1919-1939.

Typical forgeries of Loetz marks

Fake mark engraved with diamond-tip pen. All authentic engraved Loetz marks are wheel engraved. No authentic Loetz mark was engraved with a diamond-tip pen.

Fake mark engraved with vibrating electric pen. Note the typical skips particularly in the letter Z.

Loetz Austria

Fake mark engraved with diamond-tip pen.

Loetz, Austria

Loetz Austria

Two fake marks appearing as acid-stamped marks. No authentic Loetz was ever marked with acid stamps.

C.F. Monroe

C.F. Monroe was the maker of decorated art glass with white glass bodies sold under the names Wavecrest, Nakara and Kelva. Monroe was also involved in a very limited way with cut glass. Forged marks have been found in metal mountings, as well as on glass bodies.

No authentic Monroe marks were ever made with acid stamps, diamond-tip pens or engraving burrs or wheels. The vast majority of authentic marks are permanently fixed. Faked and forged marks applied by rubber stamps with ink can usually be removed with fingernail polish remover (acetone). There is no specific time period in which any of the authentic marks appeared.

There are also genuinely old wares by other makers that may be offered as C.F. Monroe. These include Keystone and Belle Ware, two lines of decorated white opaque glass made about the same time as Monroe's. Genuinely old but originally unmarked wares of all three original makers–Monroe, Keystone and Belle Ware–are the most frequent targets of forged marks.

Although best known for its white opaque glass, Monroe also produced cut glass. Original Monroe cut glass is seldom marked. The most commonly marked pieces of authentic Monroe cut glass are pieces with metal rims or metal fittings. These include covered boxes, pitchers and bowl rims. The metal was stamped C.F.M.CO. with all letters in upper case and of equal size. Authentic Monroe cut glass was never marked with acid stamps.

Authentic marks of C.F. Monroe

Original The Wavecrest "banner" mark is shown in line drawing on the left, and as a photograph, on the right. Note "The C.F.M.CO." at the bottom (white arrow). This lettering is very often blurred, filled-in or missing in forgeries of this mark. The border of authentic banner marks is made of a double-line, hollow in the middle, (black arrow) not filled-in. The original mark is about one and a quarter-inch tall.

Art Glass

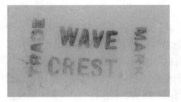

Another original Wavecrest mark. This may appear in black, brown or pink.

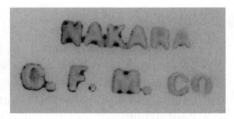

Original Nakara mark is usually black or deep brown; other colors are also possible. Also appears with Nakara on bottom line.

Original Kelva mark, usually pink; other colors possible.

Authentic mark stamped primarily in metal fittings on Monroe cut glass. These letters would never appear on glass alone. If on glass, they would always be accompanied by Nakara.

Common forgeries on C.F. Monroe

Banner mark as acid stamp. Original banners were in color, never in acid.

C.F.M.CO.

Stamped forgery in acid and ink. This mark never appears on glass by itself. It always appears on glass with Nakara. It does appear by itself stamped into genuine metal fittings, but not on glass.

KELVA

Never appears without Trade Mark on the ends (see original at top of page).

NAKARA
Never appears without C.F.M.CO either above or below.

34

Moser

Moser is art glass made by firms founded by Ludwig Moser in the middle of the 19th century which continue today. From the 1860s to 1893, Moser decorated blanks from other glass houses. Moser began making its own glass in 1893, when Moser's four sons were brought into the business.

The business went bankrupt during the 1930s and production was severely limited until the end of WW II in 1946. After the war, the company resumed production and remains in production today.

The Moser speciality was enamelling, cutting and engraving, but also includes cameo and acid etching. Moser designs have spanned many different styles of decorating including Art Nouveau, Art Deco, and Modernism.

Forgeries of Moser marks are frequently applied to new glass as well as genuinely old but unmarked wares. The most common targets are enamel decorated pieces and cut tablewares.

Authentic Moser marks

Ca. 1880-1893; applied in
gold or colored enamel.

Early cursive mark, usually
engraved, ca. 1880-1890.

Ca. 1911-1938, Ludwig Moser, Karlsbad (LMK) mono-gram in raised glass. Don't confuse this mark with the monogram of Kolo Moser, the glass designer (see Kolo Moser listing).

Ca. 1911-1938; Moser Karlsbad is a standard mark which may be in gold, colored enamel (left), raised glass (middle) or acid stamped (right). One of the most commonly forged marks.

Ca. 1926-1950; an engraved mark used throughout the 20th century until the present day. Earlier use includes acid stamp and enamel.

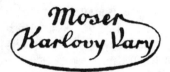

Used continously since the end of WW II, ca. 1946, as an acid stamp; Karlovy Vary is Czech for Karlsbad.

STUDIO

These two marks have been used since the mid-1990s and are applied by sandblasting.

Common Moser forgeries

Acid-etched mark with only outline of letters. No original counterpart in this style.

Fantasy cursive mark in elaborate type style; acid etched.

Two fantasy forgeries of Moser, Austria, usually acid etched. The mark on the left has also been reported in diamond-tip script. Austria never appeared in any registered Moser mark. It would be extremely rare and unusual to find "Moser, Austria" on any authentic piece of Moser.

Moser, Kolo

Austrian glass designer who worked for Loetz, Kralik and Egermann. His monogram, right, appears on some designs he made for Loetz, as well as independent work made to his designs at other firms. Usually appears as a raised glass monogram. Not to be confused with the LMK monogram of Ludwig Moser, Karlsbad (see Moser listing).

Monogram of Kolo Moser, in raised glass.

Mount Washington Glass Co.

The origins of Mount Washington date back to 1837. It was well known for its decorative art glass throughout the 19th century. In 1894, the company merged with Pairpoint. Two of its most famous lines, Royal Flemish and Crown Milano, are listed under their own entries in this chapter. A cut glass line, Russian Crystal, is listed in the Cut Glass chapter.

Genuine This original trademark was used on paper labels only.

No authentic items are marked Mount Washington directly on the glass. If pieces are marked, they are usually with the name of the particular line such as Royal Flemish or Crown Milano. The Mount Washington trademark, shown above, was used on paper labels only, never on glass. Similar original paper labels have variations in wording incorporating the various line names (see Royal, Flemish, etc.). The basic circular trademark shown here has been forged with an acid stamp. A forgery with a block-letter stamp has been seen in acid and various colors of ink.

Pairpoint

The Pairpoint Manufacturing Co. was founded in 1880 and initially made metal castings. In 1894, Pairpoint merged with the Mount Washington Glass Co. and continued on as Pairpoint Corp. until 1938.

Pairpoint Corp., operating 1894-1938, never put "Pairpoint" on table glass or on art glass. Forgers often copy trademarks and company logos they find in reference books without understanding the original use. The original ca. 1894-1938 trademark of the letter P in a diamond, for example, was only used on paper labels, as artwork in company advertisements or stamped in metal. It was never used as a permanent mark on pre-1938 table or art glass. Any appearance of the P-diamond mark on glass offered as pre-1938 is automatically suspect.

The script Pairpoint trademark is also commonly reproduced. Like the P-diamond, the script Pairpoint trademark was never used on pre-1938 glass. It was primarily used in advertising material and catalogs, but not on glass.

Another common forgery often found on lamp shades is Pairpoint

Art Glass

MFG. Co. That particular lettering is an authentic mark, but the authentic version was used only as a stamped mark in metal; it never appeared on authentic Pairpoint glass shades.

Authentic Pairpoint marks

The Pairpoint Corp'n is the authentic stamped ink mark on pre-1938 Pairpoint glass shade. Usually in dark brown or black. Always includes the word "The" and the unusual abbreviation of corporation, "Corp'n.," with an apostrophe and the letter "n."

Authentic ca. 1916-1938 paper label; black ink on white paper. Brought back in identical appearance by Gunderson-Pairpoint 1952-1957.

Paper label ca. 1952-1957, Gunderson-Pairpoint Glass Works, black ink on white label.

Letter P inside diamond has been handpainted or etched with a diamond tip pencil since ca. 1970s. Generally quite small, usually under three-eighths inch tall.

P in diamond appears in some pressed glass cup plates made since 1974. A P in diamond does not appear in any pre-1938 glass.

PAIRPOINT

3806

Authentic Pairpoint mark stamped in metal. Includes "Pairpoint MFG.Co." and letter P inside a diamond. The diamond is fairly consistent in almost all marks in metal. A variety of other words may appear together with the P and diamond such as "quadruple plate" and "New Bedford Mass."

P in diamond with shape number and Pairpoint above found on painted metal only, not on glass.

E.P.N.S. is an authentic mark on Pairpoint silverplate, an abbreviation for Electro Plate on Nickel Silver. The mark W.M. Mounts designates white metal mountings. Pieces with the WM mark are sometimes mistakenly offered as Mount Washington silver. Mount Washington Glass, which made fine art glass, merged with Pairpoint in 1894. For related marks, see "Mount Washington" later in this chapter.

E.P.N.S.
W.M.MOUNTS

Common Pairpoint forgeries

P in diamond, usually appearing as an acid-etched mark on cut glass. This is an authentic Pairpoint trademark but it was never used on pre-1938 glass. It was stamped in metal.

Pairpoint script mark has been found as ink stamp on shades and as an acid-stamped mark on a variety of cut and decorated glass. This mark was never used on any glass.

PAIRPOINT MFG. CO.

Seen as an acid-etched mark and also stamped in ink on shades. This particular wording was stamped into metal only; it was never applied to any authentic pre-1928 cut or art glass or glass shade.

Reproduction three-inch Gundersen burmese vase. Marked with diamond pen, P inside diamond.

QUEZAL

Quezal Art Glass and Decorating Co. was started in 1901 by Martin Bach and Thomas Johnson. Both Bach and Johnson were former Tiffany employees and familiar with Tiffany's glass formulas and decorating techniques. Most Quezal was very similar in finish and shape to Tiffany. It's estimated that about 80-90 percent of all Quezal production was in the form of lamp shades. The company failed and went out of business by 1924.

Most Quezal in general and shades in particular were marked. Virtually all marks were engraved with a wheel. Quezal wheel engraved marks have a distinctive pattern in the letters of tightly grouped, uniformly spaced, parallel horizontal lines. Most genuine marks on shades appear on the inside of the fitter rim. Many genuine Quezal marks engraved on white glass bodies were rubbed with either black or silver producing black or silver horizontal lines in the mark. Original marks vary in size.

Any piece marked Quezal with a matte acid stamp, engraved with a ball-shaped rotary bit or engraved with a diamond-tip stylus is almost certain to be a forgery.

Genuine Typical wheel-engraved Quezal mark streaked with horizontal gaps in the form of fine lines.

Genuine Typical Quezal wheel-engraved mark on inside of fitter rim.

Fake Any matte-acid Quezal mark is a forgery. No original Quezal was ever marked with acid stamps.

Fake Any engraved Quezal mark made with a ball-shaped bit or diamond-tip stylus is almost certainly a forgery.

Royal Flemish

Royal Flemish was a line of art glass made by Mt. Washington Glass Co. ca. 1893. Original mark of F and reversed R is handpainted and slightly irregular; color is usually red or reddish brown. The FR may also appear without the diamond. Most fake marks are rubber stamped.

The round Royal Flemish mark appeared as a paper label only. Forgeries of this mark have been seen in indelible ink and acid stamped. Any mark on glass of this mark is a forgery.

Forgery New marks are rubber stamped in acid or ink.

Genuine Original mark was hand-painted. Brush strokes are obvious.

Genuine This mark appeared on paper labels only. If you find this mark applied directly to the glass, it's a forgery.

Art Glass

Smith Brothers

The Smith Brothers, Alfred and Harry, began decorating glass with their father at the Boston and Sandwich Glass Company in the 1850s. In the early 1870s, the brothers began a decorating shop at Mount Washington Glass. Later, in 1874, the brothers bought out the shop and began their own firm, Smith Brothers. The company went bankrupt in 1899.

Far from all original Smith Brothers glass was marked. The most common mark is the rampant lion and shield which was stamped in reddish brown, rust-colored ink. Handpainted marks were also used. Of these, Smith Bros signed in script usually appears in black paint.

The typical forgeries are applied with rubber stamps. The rampant lion is the most frequent forgery because it is the best known. Most forged lion marks are blotchy with filled in letters, gaps in lines and generally very ragged. Sure, original lion marks may have a few slight irregularities and, to a certain extent, some flaws are to be expected. But be logical. Would the same shop, famous for applying delicate enamel tracery and hair-thin gold piping by hand, have a problem operating a rubber stamp? Not likely.

Genuine Smith Bros. handpainted mark. Although painted in script, note that the letters are not linked or joined. This is typical of many Smith Bros. handpainted marks. This example and most, but not all, other handpainted marks are in black.

Genuine Smith Bros. rampant lion and shield mark was stamped in reddish brown ink.

Common Smith Bros. forgeries

Smith Bros. CO
TRADE-MARK

Smith Bros. Co

SMITH BROS. CO
TRADE-MARK

Forgeries Three rubber-stamped fantasy marks, no old counterparts existed. Seen in acid and black ink.

Forgery A new mark applied with a rubber stamp and red ink.

Steuben

Steuben Glass Works was founded in 1903 in Corning, New York. Led by Frederick Carder, the firm began making iridescent glass in the Art Nouveau styles similar to Tiffany. Steuben continued to make high-quality colored art glass until 1932. In 1932, colored glass was discontinued and Steuben turned to producing clear crystal only, which remains the glass it makes today.

Reproductions are getting more sophisticated and are now frequently made in original shapes. Forged Steuben marks are also improving and often include model numbers that correspond to the original shape.

Generally, original iridescent Steuben Aurene should feel silky smooth over the entire surface. Many reproductions have rough, pitted surfaces that feel coarse. Original iridescence is consistent over the entire surface. That means the underside of the base looks about the same as the sides of a vase. Many reproductions will not have iridescence on the undersides of bases.

All original Steuben pontils are polished without exception. Most reproductions with forged marks have rough pontils. It is not unusual, though, for unethical sellers to polish out new rough pontils to create an imitation of an original piece. Marks on legitimate new studio glass in Art Nouveau styles–like Orient and Flume, Lundberg Studios, and others–are also frequently ground out before applying forged marks.

Authentic engraved marks

Steuben's line of iridescent art glass, named Aurene, was made from 1904 to 1932. Most, but not all, Aurene is marked either Aurene or Steuben Aurene and usually located around ground pontils. The vast majority of authentic marks on Aurene are engraved. Aurene or Steuben Aurene should never appear as acid-etched marks or be applied by the thin tip of a diamond pencil or electric vibrating pen. Authentic marks tend to be irregular and slightly wavy in appearance. Original engraved marks are usually, but not always, followed by a

Genuine Original engraved marks usually appear around the pontil. Authentic engraved marks have a rough, "shaky" appearance. Used ca. 1904-1932.

Art Glass

catalog shape number. Authentic marks vary considerably in size of letters, style and technique.

Authentic fleur-de-lis marks

Original acid fleur-de-lis marks were used between 1903 and 1932. An authentic acid-stamped fleur-de-lis is only about three-eighths-inch tall. Forged marks are almost always much larger; many up to an inch tall. Many faked marks are made up of areas filled in acid with only the letters left clear. In the original mark, only the outline of the fleur-de-lis and the letters are in matte acid. Fleur-de-lis marks never appear on authentic clear colorless Steuben made after 1932.

The small original fleur-de-lis was also used on Steuben art glass lamp shades, primarily those with two and one-quarter inch fitter rims. For those marks, powdered metal was added to the acid to produce a fleur-de-lis silvery in color rather than colorless matte acid. These marks appear on the inside of the fitter rim. Most, but not all, original marks were applied with the point of the fleur-de-lis pointing towards the inside of the shade.

   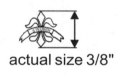

actual size 3/8"

Genuine Authentic fleur-de-lis mark is formed by lines etched in acid. Original marks are quite small, about three-eighths inch tall. Used ca. 1904-1932 on wide variety of colored glass. This mark should not appear on any iridescent glass.

Steuben art glass shade with two and one-quarter inch fitter rim, left. Silvery Steuben fleur-de-lis marks on fitter rims generally point towards inside of shade, upper right. An original silver fleur-de-lis may show considerable wear and some blurring as this example, right.

Genuine These fleur-de-lis marks are in raised glass produced by cutting back the surrounding areas with acid. Used ca. 1915-1932.

Unlike genuine matte acid fleur-de-lis marks, which are virtually always sharp and clean, original silver fleur-de-lis marks on shades are often badly blurred with the letters sometimes filled in. It is also common to find the silver fleur-de-lis on shades badly worn and showing considerable wear. The silver fleur-de-lis is sometimes forged with mixtures made from silver paint. These forgeries are usually very pebbly in appearance and can be rubbed off with a fingernail. Original silver fleur-de-lis marks are usually very smooth and, although subject to gradual wear, cannot easily be removed. Even with the silver badly worn on an original mark, a shadow of the mark virtually always remains and can be seen with a 10X loupe.

As a general rule, genuine Steuben shades with two and one-quarter inch fitter rims should never be marked with the matte acid fleur-de-lis nor with an engraved mark such as Aurene or Steuben.

Acid was also used to produce two *raised* fleur-de-lis marks with either STEUBEN or CALCITE on the banner. The background was etched away leaving the mark in three-dimensional relief, a technique called "acid cutback" (ACB). These raised marks usually appear on the base, but can also appear in other locations. Raised marks began to be used around 1915 when Calcite, a white-bodied glass, was introduced.

Other authentic acid marks

Around 1929, three new styles of acid marks began to be used. One of the first was a rectangular box with the copyright symbol ©, the

Genuine Three acid-stamped marks introduced around 1929. From left: C.G.W. Corning Glass Works, block lettering mark, script style.

Art Glass

year 1929 and the initials C.G.W. for Corning Glass Works. There was another, simpler style in block letters and the third version was a script style. Generally, but not always, these transition marks appeared on the clear colorless glass designs that began to evolve in the late 1920s. All three of these marks were applied as an acid stamp. Like genuine fleur-de-lis marks used earlier, these acid marks are generally well-formed, uniformly consistent and virtually never appear with blurred or filled-in letters. These three principle marks continued to be used after 1932 until they were gradually replaced by marks applied with diamond-tip pencils, shown next.

Post-1932 engraved marks

As colorless glass replaced earlier colored-glass lines, marks also changed. Standard production colorless Steuben made since 1932 is generally marked with a diamond-tip pencil or stylus. The diamond-tip marks are quite small, rarely over one-eighth to three-sixteenth inches tall; generally under one-inch long. Marks made with a diamond-tip stylus were not used on Steuben wares made before ca. 1930.

Steuben   S

Genuine The standard Steuben marks on colorless glass made since 1932 are applied with a diamond-tip stylus. Marks after 1932 are very small; the full word Steuben is usually about three-quarters inch long and rarely over one-inch long.

Questionable engraved marks Frederick Carder engraved his name and sometimes dates on glass brought to him by the general public until Carder's death in 1963 at age 100. Some of these signatures are very large, some measuring several inches wide. No F. Carder script signature was ever applied at the time of production to standard Steuben art glass made ca. 1903-1930. The only documented pieces dated and signed F. Carder in script at the time of production are pieces of Diatreta made 1949-1959.

Typical fake and forged Steuben marks

Forgeries Blurred acid-stamp fleur-de-lis mark, left, is typical of most acid forgeries. Forgery on right is reversed from original stamp; segments of fleur-de-lis are blurred together.

Forgers have become more sophisticated and are reproducing original shapes and marking them with original shape numbers. Photo on the left shows shape number 2564 from the original Steuben catalog; the reproduction is shown in center. The forged mark on the reproduction includes the correct shape number 2564, right. Although correct shape numbers can help confirm an original mark, shape numbers alone are no guarantee of authenticity.

A   **B**   **C**

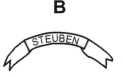
steuben

Common acid-etched fakes A)– A reverse version of the original fleur-de-lis acid mark; B)– Banner alone was never acid etched; C) an acid-etched version of post-1930 Steuben script mark.

Art Glass

Stevens and Williams

Stevens and Williams is one of England's finest glass houses dating back to 1847 and located in Stourbridge. Among its famous glass makers were Harry Northwood and his son, Harry II, and Frederick Carder who started Steuben Glass in America.

Stevens and Williams made fine colored glass including cameo throughout the Victorian era. Some of its finer pieces were marked with a fleur-de-lis with the initials S and W on either side. England often appears in a banner below. This mark can appear as an acid-stamped mark or in raised glass on cameo pieces. Other marks on cameo are often the company name arranged in a circle and etched below the surface.

After the 1920s, the firm turned its production to clear stemware for the table. The name was changed to Brierley Glassware and later, Royal Brierley.

Genuine Acid stamped, ca. 1902-1930.

Genuine Etched in relief on bases.

Forgery A retooled Steuben fleur-de-lis with an S and W added. Acid stamped. Actual size is about one-half inch tall.

S & W Patent

Forgery Fantasy acid-stamped mark. Actual size is a little over one inch.

Tchécoslovaquie

Tchécoslovaquie is the French spelling of Czechoslovakia. This mark was used on Czech goods made specifically for the French market. The frosted glass example shown has the word molded on the bottom of a vase.

Tchécoslovaquie is French for Czechoslovakia. This mark can be found on pieces made in Czechoslovakia, ca. 1919-1939.

Tiffany

Louis Comfort Tiffany (1848 to 1933) was a leading designer of the Art Nouveau period. He is perhaps best known for his art glass and table lamps, but also designed jewelry, metalwork, textiles, pottery, and complete interiors. Although his name appears on most objects, Tiffany himself never worked on any glass or lamps. All work was performed by highly skilled artisans according to Tiffany's designs.

Before 1890, most objects were custom-made for special commissions in Tiffany's interior design business and marks on those pieces varied greatly. After 1890, more goods were made for the general public, and those are the majority of pieces in the market today.

Forged signature "L. C. Tiffany Favrile 3343B." Found on this new 11-inch blue iridescent vase.

Tiffany glass date codes

Marks before 1892 used numbers only. After 1893, letters were added before the number (prefix). From 1906 on, letters were added after the number (suffix).

Examples: E/2458 = 1896 789/Q=1922

From 1 to 9999, 1892-1893

pr A or B, 1894	sf A, 1906	sf M, 1918
pr C or D, 1895	sf B, 1907	sf N, 1919
pr E or F, 1896	sf C, 1908	sf O, 1920
pr G or H, 1897	sf D, 1909	sf P, 1921
pr I or J, 1898	sf E, 1910	sf Q, 1922
pr K or L, 1899	sf F, 1911	sf R, 1923
pr M or N, 1900	sf G, 1912	sf S, 1924
pr O or P, 1901	sf H, 1913	sf T, 1925
pr Q or R, 1902	sf I, 1914	sf U, 1926
pr S or T, 1903	sf J, 1915	sf V, 1927
pr U or V, 1904	sf K, 1916	sf W, 1928
pr W or Y, 1905	sf L, 1917	

All production of Tiffany products ended in 1938.

Tiffany's companies operated under various names over the years, and these are reflected in the marks. There are so many Tiffany marks that it is particularly important to understand which marks were originally used on the various materials. Some original marks appear only on metal, others only on glass. Some of today's forgeries are trademarks that only appeared on legal documents and were never used as marks.

The most common forgeries of Tiffany marks are found on iridescent art glass. Original engraved marks appear on Tiffany blown glass made from 1893 to 1928. There are many differences found among original engraved marks. Some are illegible, others are in beautiful flowing script. Marks on original iridescent pieces are almost always rotary-engraved. Some pieces were marked with only a

Forged Tiffany "TGDCO" paper label. Very poor lettering, black on white paper. Irregular wavy edge from hand cutting; about five-eighths inch diameter.

Forged "LCT" monogram paper label. Black lettering on white paper. Hand cut wavy edge on label; about three-quarter inch diameter. Original shown below.

Authentic LCT monogram paper label. Embossed gold printing on green background on white paper. Original labels are only about three-quarter inch diameter. Shown here on polished pontil with authentic engraved mark. Note the small size of original engraved letters.

diamond-tip stylus but these are mostly the later pastel pieces. Most, but not all, original engraved marks include model numbers or date codes (see chart). Keep in mind, however, that clever forgers know all about date and shape codes and will include those numbers in faked marks.

Large, poorly spaced, badly proportioned or awkwardly located marks are always suspect. Original engraved marks are usually only three sixteenths to one quarter-inch tall on even the largest pieces. Any

Art Glass

acid-etched Tiffany mark is a fake. No original Tiffany glass was ever marked with acid. Many of the acid fakes are copied from trademarks and logos that were originally used in stationery, patent applications and advertising only, never as a mark on glass.

Faked paper labels have been increasing in recent years. It's a relatively simple matter to make paper labels on home computers with image editing software and high quality printers. The vast majority of new paper labels fluoresce under black light. Many marks used on the new paper labels were never used on original paper labels.

Typical authentic Tiffany marks on glass

Authentic engraved marks were made with a variety of methods including small wheels, ball-shaped bits and a diamond-tip stylus. There is very wide variation in appearance among originals. Many, but not all, Tiffany marks are followed by date codes. Generally, most signatures are placed in or around ground pontils. Most engraved marks have a jagged or shaky appearance. Engraved marks are rarely over one-quarter inch in height.

Authentic TGDC monogram (Tiffany Glass Decorating Co); paper label used 1890s to 1902. Rarely found, but a possibility.

LCT monogram used on paper labels after 1902. There are many forgeries of this mark in black and white paper. Most new paper fluoresces under long wave black light.

Common Tiffany forgeries

Typical forged Tiffany engraved signature. Very large half-inch tall letters extend halfway around the base. The great majority of original marks appear around the ground pontil in letters rarely over one-quarter inch tall. This fake includes a date mark, A-1031, for the year 1894. A very deep round-bottom trench-like engraving typical of those made with modern carbide or diamond tip ball-shaped burrs. Many tools are used to engrave forged marks. The marks various modern tools leave are shown in close up photos at the beginning of this section.

1.    **2.**

All five of these marks shown here have been found as acid stamps. No authentic Tiffany art glass was ever marked with acid stamps. The two top marks have been copied from the artwork on trademark applications; neither was ever used in any form to mark glass. The bottom three are simply variations of type styles ordered as rubber stamps from office supply stores.

3.

L. C. T. Favrile

4.

**TIFFANY STUDIOS
NEW YORK**

5. L.C. TIFFANY CO.

Art Glass

Webb Corbett, Ltd.

Originally known as White House Glassworks, transferred to Thomas Webb III in 1897 under the name of Thomas Webb & Corbett, Ltd. The name was shortened to Webb, Corbett Ltd. in the 1930s. Absorbed by the Royal Doulton Group in 1969. The main production of Webb Corbett, Ltd. since the 1930s has been cut stemware. Most pieces are marked by sandblasting or acid stamping.

In the 1970s, Webb Corbett brought back a limited line of modern cameo glass. The new pieces were called "air carved," another name for sandblasting. These pieces had a single layer of colored glass over a thick clear glass body.

It should be kept in mind that even pre-1925 Webb Corbett is not as highly valued as products from Thomas Webb & Sons. Some care needs to be taken to avoid confusing the marks of Webb Corbett with those of Thomas Webb.

Original mark registered 1897.

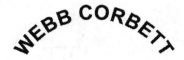

These two marks used on cut stemware, ca. 1930-1960.

Contemporary mark; S designates the factory at Stourbridge.

Contemporary mark, T represents factory at Tutbury.

 Acid-etched fake script mark.

Thomas Webb & Sons

The Webb family has been a famous name in English glass since the 18th century. The best known branch of the family begins with John Webb and the White House Glass Works in the 1830s. John passed this glass works to his son Thomas Webb I in 1835. Thomas went on to found Thomas Webb & Sons, which operated several glass houses known as Dennis Glassworks. When Thomas I retired in 1863, he was succeeded by three sons, Thomas II, Charles and Walter. In 1919, the Dennis Glass Works was reorganized under the name Webb's Crystal Glass Co. Ltd. Another merger in 1964 combined the original Thomas Webb & Sons and Webb's Crystal Glass under the name Crown House Ltd.

Thomas Webb & Sons produced some of the world's finest Victorian art glass including cameo, cut and colored wares. When most people speak of Webb, they are generally referring to the products of Thomas Webb & Sons made ca. 1870-1919. Many pieces of Webb–particularly Webb cameo–are among the most highly priced pieces in the market. Forgeries have been reported since the mid-1960s and they are becoming increasingly more common (see Webb cameo marks in the Cameo chapter of this book).

Authentic marks of Thomas Webb & Sons

Acid-etched relief
ca. 1906 to ca.1935.

Acid-etched relief
ca. 1936 to ca.1949.

Acid-etched relief
ca. 1950 to ca.1966.

THOS
WEBB
ENGLAND
Sandblasted
ca. 1966 to ca.1980.

THOMAS
WEBB
ENGLAND
Sandblasted
since 1980.

Genuine Two examples of acid cutback marks on Webb's Burmese, Queens Burmese Ware, Patented, Thos. Webb & Sons. The marks may appear with letters either below the surface, left, or raised above the surface, right. Used 1887 to ca. 1913. May or may not also include the English Registry number, 81067, which is the only correct number that appears with genuine Webb Burmese marks.

Photograph of Webb Queens Burmese acid cutback mark with Registry number 81067. These acid cutback original marks vary considerably in clarity and sharpness. This mark is typical

This trademark remained in registration through the 1960s. Exact use not confirmed; believed to be used on paper labels.

Marks often incorrectly attributed to Thomas Webb and Sons

So-called propeller mark handpainted in black enamel. It is widely thought in the American market that this is a mark of Thomas Webb and Sons. Research by Robert and Deborah Truitt have positively traced this mark to Harrach, a major Bohemian glass factory since the early 18th century. The mark is derived from the Harrach family coat of arms. Forgeries (see below) are still offered as Webb.

So-called spider web mark in handpainted red and sometimes black enamel. Widely represented as Thomas Webb & Sons but never actually proved. It is English and dates to late 19th-early 20th century, but exact source not established. However, it's often forged and offered as Webb, see example below.

Common forgeries of Thomas Webb and Sons

WEBB

WEBB-PATENT

Three typical samples of rubber stamped forgeries. These stamps have been found in matte acid, as well as indelible ink applied to opaque glass. There are no old counterparts to these rubber-stamped marks.

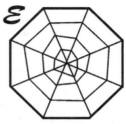

Forgery Crude propeller rubber stamped in black and red ink and sometimes matte acid. Found on colored opaque and clear glass.

Forgery Rubber-stamped mark in indelible ink with straight rigid lines. Originals were always handpainted.

57

Cameo Glass

Group of cameo reproductions, four to eight inches tall. Signed in raised cameo, from left: Richard, Thomas Webb, Muller.

Reproduction cameo glass marked "Gallé" has been in the market since at least 1993. Until recently, it was thought that Gallé was the only significant mark appearing on cameo reproductions.

Since mid-1999, however, marks from other well-known original cameo glass manufacturers have been appearing on reproductions of both French and English cameo glass. These include Thomas Webb, Daum Nancy, Richard, Legras, Muller and Schneider.

Many buyers–believing cameo reproductions were marked Gallé

only– never suspected other marks were being copied and have paid significant prices for new pieces with names of other makers. Virtually all marks of all original makers have been reproduced.

Most new marks are virtually identical to original marks in size, appearance and method of manufacture. Like the originals they copy, most new marks are in raised lettering formed by removing the surrounding background. Marks by themselves are not a reliable test of age or authenticity. Studying and understanding how original cameo glass was made is the best way to detect the reproductions.

You should also attempt to learn how specific original marks were applied. Many reference books on cameo glass, for example, show original marks and signatures only as line drawings. There are very few published photos of authentic marks. If you try to look up marks for La Verre Francais, for example, most reference books illustrate the original mark as a line drawing. Forgers, using the line drawings to guide them, have reproduced Le Verre Francais as a raised glass mark. All original marks were engraved or etched below the surface, never raised glass.

Many authentic marks are shown only as line drawings in reference books. Forgers copy many of these marks without knowing which original marks appeared as letters of raised glass or letters engraved or etched below the surface. Knowing how original marks appeared can very often help determine whether a suspected mark is authentic or a forgery. The book shown here is *French Cameo Glass*, Blount, © 1968, one of the standard reference works on cameo glass. The mark on every piece of glass photographed in the book is listed in the back.

Cameo Glass

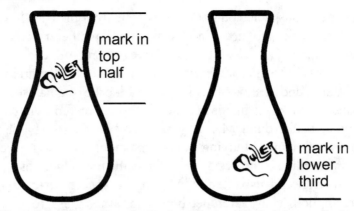

mark in top half

mark in lower third

New marks are much more prominent than originals. Most marks in original French cameo are in the lower third of an object. Many new marks are placed in the top half of a piece.

Location can also be a clue to new and forged marks on cameo reproductions. Generally, most new marks are placed in locations far more conspicuous than original marks. Most marks on reproductions of French cameo, for example, are located somewhere in the top half of the piece on which they appear. The vast majority of original marks were much more subtle and less obvious, usually appearing around the bottom of a piece usually in the lower third.

A brochure from 1993 offering new cameo glass signed "Gallé."

60

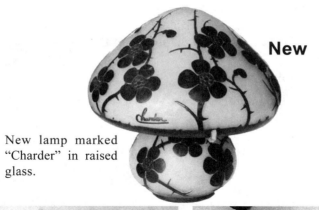

New

New lamp marked
"Charder" in raised
glass.

 **New**

 **Old**

Charder

A series of new lamps is marked "Charder" in raised glass. The new marks are close copies of the original raised glass Charder mark. The original Charder was a trade name of Schneider Glass Co., France, produced 1917 to 1932. Virtually all original pieces of Charder are also marked Le Verre Francais, which is engraved or etched.

The Charder mark on the new lamps is very thick and heavy. Original Charder was made with a nearly paper thin overlay. It was this overlay that was cut back to form the original mark (also see Le Verre Francais in this section).

Ciriama

This mark is found on pieces made with a core of clear body glass with paper thin colored layers on either side. An example is shown in Blount, *French Cameo Glass*, © 1968, but without mention of age.

Very thin raised glass
mark found Ciriama.
Exact age unknown,
probably mid- to late-
1930s.

Cameo Glass

The source or date of production for pieces with this name have never been fully identified. Production attributed to the last years of vintage cameo production, ca. 1930s.

Vase marked Ciriama.

Cristvo (cristuo?)

Found on reproduction cameo glass from eastern Europe. No old counterpart known.

Daum Nancy

New cameo glass vase with raised glass "Daum Nancy" signature. New mark is virtually identical to original raised glass marks. Original Daum Nancy marks may be applied in many different methods–raised glass, engraved, enameled or etched.

Raised glass "Daum Nancy" signature found on a new 11-inch vase.

de Vianne

De Vianne raised glass signature on new multilayer cameo glass made in France, especially lamps and lamp shades. De Vianne paper labels also found on Lalique-style frosted glassware.

D'Aurys

See Kralik entry in this chapter.

Gallé

New Gallé marks on reproduction cameo vary widely in appearance. Many new Gallé marks are virtually identical in general appearance to original marks.

Reproductions marked Gallé and TIP were first made in Romania about 1993. These first pieces were fairly good quality and well-made. TIP is Romanian meaning "type" or "in the manner of." TIP was a legal warning that the piece was not genuine Gallé, but "in the style of Gallé." Many times TIP marks are explained away by sellers as a "student" of Gallé or a gallery that sold Gallé glass. Many pieces originally marked TIP have had the TIP letters ground away, leaving only the Gallé mark.

TIP and Gallé marks are usually, but not always, fairly close together as shown in a typical mark above. The exact position, size and appearance vary from piece to piece. The mark above appears on the 12-inch lamp at left, which is a high-quality reproduction from Romania.

TIP styles vary considerably in appearance and size. No TIP mark was ever used on pre-1930 cameo.

Cameo Glass

Typical raised glass "Gallé" mark on inexpensive cameo glass reproduction made in China, ca. 1999. Wholesale price for average 6-inch new vases with Gallé marks in 1999 was $50.

Reproduction of a Gallé mold blown, or "blown out" 10-inch vase. A prominent raised glass "Gallé" signature appears on the side.

Kralik

The Austrian glass works of Wilhelm Kralik Söhn produced inexpensive generic cameo for foreign wholesale importers. These pieces were marked with various coined names in a French style. Two of these names were D'Aurys and Soleil.

Legras

New raised glass mark on reproduction cameo glass. New marks appear in various forms and sizes. This mark on a five and one-half inch vase.

Le Verre Francais

The original Le Verre Francais was one of the lines of glass created and manufactured by the Schneider Glass Co. of France. All

Old

Authentic Le Verre Francais mark engraved below the surface.

original Le Verre Francais marks are engraved or etched *below* the surface of the glass, not raised above the surface.

Authentic Le Verre Francais marks also appear on glass marked Charder which was another line of Schneider glass. On Charder pieces, the Charder name appeared in acid cutback raised glass, but the Le Verre Francais name was engraved, or etched, not raised.

In addition to the engraved mark or in place of an engraved mark, a rod of white glass with colored glass stripes–the so-called candy cane mark–may be embedded in the surface. This cane is an authentic mark of Schneider glass used in Le Verre Francais.

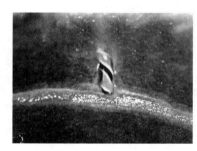

Old

One of the authentic marks on Le Verre Francais is this rod of white glass with colored glass stripes embedded in the surface of the glass. This is referred to as the candy cane mark. It usually, but not always, appears in the side of a piece rather than the bottom.

New

"Le Verre Francais" appears in raised glass on some new pieces of cameo. All authentic Le Verre Francais marks are engraved or etched below the surface, not raised.

Loetz

Increasing interest in glass of eastern Europe has led to many discoveries about the products of Loetz. Robert and Deborah Truitt have been among the first Americans to do extensive research in the Czech Republic, Austria and parts of Germany. The Truitts and other authors are gradually documenting a more accurate picture of the extent and nature of the glass made by Loetz and other firms.

Loetz, for example, made very little cameo compared to the large French firms of Gallé, Daum and Pantine. Loetz cameo can be divided into two groups: 1) pieces marketed as Loetz products with the Loetz name; and, 2) cameo produced as "private labels" and generic

Cameo Glass

products for wholesale importers around the world.

Cameo pieces sold as Loetz products were generally marked Loetz in raised glass, usually in script. The mark of a glass designer may or may not accompany the Loetz mark somewhere on the piece (also see the Loetz entry in the Art Glass chapter).

Beginning around 1920, Loetz began supplying French-styled cameo to glass wholesalers around the world. The great majority of these products were inexpensive two-color pieces with a single acid cutting. In one of the most surprising developments in Bohemian glass research, the Truitts have found many marks and names long associated with French cameo makers were actually trade names developed and used by Loetz. Some of these names include Veles, Velez, and Richard. These mass-produced pieces with French-appearing marks were made and sold, ca. 1921-1928.

Virtually all books on antique glass that include cameo–including Blount's *French Cameo,* the standard reference on the subject–incorrectly identify Loetz's "French" trade names. Kralik, another Bohemian glass house, also made cameo with French-sounding names (see Kralik entry in this chapter).

High-quality cameo glass sold under the Loetz name was usually marked Loetz in raised script. Exact appearance varies; may also include the mark of a glass designer. Used ca. 1900-1920s.

Loetz cameo made expressly for the American market is marked Ca. Loetz in raised glass. Used ca. 1922-1925.

Two of the French-styled names used by Loetz were Veles, left, and Velez, right. Both appear as raised glass marks, ca. 1922-1925.

Forgery

Richard has long been assumed and is recorded in most books as a separate French cameo maker. It is actually one of the names registered by Loetz, ca. 1922-1925. Appears in raised glass. There is considerable variation among old marks.

Richard is so firmly regarded as a French mark, it is among the mass-produced cameo fakes commonly found in today's market. This raised glass Richard mark is found on a 6-inch reproduction cameo vase made in China. New Richard marks are virtually identical to old.

Muller

Two new raised glass "Muller" marks. Virtually identical to original Muller marks.

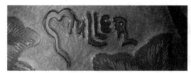

Ramski

Ryszard Ramski is a contemporary Polish glassmaker. Raised glass mark shown here is found on cameo-style glass produced in the early 1990s. Examples shown here range in size from three and one-half inches to eleven inches. Decorations include praying mantis, humming bird, butterflies and florals. The group shown here was made in 1993 and retailed from $145 to $325.

Cameo Glass

Richard See Loetz entry in this chapter.

Schneider

New raised glass mark, "Schneider." Virtually all authentic Schneider marks are engraved or etched, not raised glass. Any Schneider mark in raised glass is almost certainly a reproduction or forgery (also see Le Verre Francais and Charder in this section).

Soleil See Kralik entry in this chapter.

Tudor

Found on new cameo glass made in Bistrita, Romania, ca. early 1990s. The mark appears as raised glass. Exported worldwide through a national Romanian trade office, Industrial Central for Glass and Ceramics(CISCF). Possibly copied from a trade name of the Stourbridge Glass Co., Stourbridge, England. The Stourbridge Tudor appeared in an Old English type style.

Raised glass mark on reproduction cameo

Stourbridge Glass trade name that appears etched on some cut wares.

Thomas Webb and Sons

The authentic examples shown on the next page are the most common, but certainly not all, of the authentic marks found on Thomas Webb and Sons cameo made ca. 1880 to 1910.

None of these marks would ever appear as a simple matte acid stamp. Sharpness of detail varies considerably among original marks. Generally, Webb cameo was marked on the bottom, not the sides as French cameo was marked. The only Webb cameo consistently marked on the side is the so-called pseudo cameo, made in the 1930s. Other than that exception, it would be unusual to find any of the genuine marks shown here on the side of an authentic piece.

Original Thomas Webb & Sons cameo marks

Thomas Webb & Sons circular marks found on bases only. One version with CAMEO, left; the same with PATENT, right.

Thomas Webb & Sons in semi-circular banner. Gem Cameo or Cameo may appear below.

Semi-circular banner variation with no secondary mark.

Left Webb in shell-style background, a registration number may appear below. This mark always on the bottom.

Script raised glass mark on pseudo cameo, a 1930s inexpensive alternative to Webb's Victorian cameo.

Typical forgeries on Thomas Webb & Sons cameo

Acid cutback mark first found in 1990. No original counterpart to this mark is known.

Very crude raised glass "THOS WEBB & SONS, LTD" mark on the side of a reproduction cameo vase made in China. The mark is formed at the factory.

Cut Glass

Several years ago, an advanced collector of cut glass I spoke with estimated as much as 30-40 percent of the signed cut glass he was offered had recently applied marks. Either there were new marks on new glass, new marks on genuinely old but originally unmarked glass or new marks that did not match the company known to have made a particular shape or pattern (a Libbey mark on a known Hawkes pattern for example).

The collector went on to say that almost all desirable old cut glass can fairly easily be attributed to specific companies by the pattern and shape of the blanks. "About the only people interested in acid stamped marks," he concluded, "are beginning cut glass collectors or dealers that handle a general line. As long as someone is willing to pay extra for a marked piece, unethical people will fill that demand by applying forged marks."

Where do these forgeries come from? It's relatively easy to put new marks on cut glass. All you need is a rubber stamp and some acid, or etching fluid. Rubber stamps can be made at almost any office supply store for $10-$20. Etching fluids can be purchased at most craft stores.

Slightly more advanced methods involve producing a negative image of a mark in a rub-on acrylic material similar to the press-on letters you buy in sheets. This material is so flexible it can wrap around curves and create marks in areas impossible to mark with the rigid rubber stamps. It can produce very high quality images with extremely fine lines. After the acid is applied, the material rinses off without a trace.

One of the easiest ways to identify new marks on cut glass is to be aware of what marks were actually used as stamps. Many of the marks shown in cut glass reference books are simply trademarks used in advertising or letterheads and never appeared as acid marks on glass. Still other marks were used as paper labels only. If any of these marks is found as an acid stamp, it is automatically a forgery.

The best way to avoid forged marks, though, is to refuse to pay higher prices for marked examples. Without a demand, forged marks would become far less common.

Most forged marks on cut glass are in matte acid applied with rubber stamps.

A slightly higher-tech method of applying new marks is with a stencil made of a rub-on material. The acid will penetrate the open areas and the black mask will be rinsed away. This new material can be wrapped around curved surfaces.

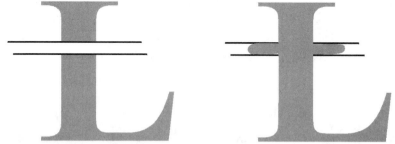

Genuinely old marks applied at the time of manufacture will logically show scratches produced by normal wear. In other words, scratches will go through original marks, as shown above left. Many new marks applied to old but originally unmarked pieces will often be placed over scratches. Under a 10X loupe, you can usually see the acid in these new marks flowing into the old scratches, above right.

Cut Glass

All marks acid etched unless stated otherwise.

C.G. Alford Co
N Y, NY, ca. 1872-1918.

M.J. Averbeck
Honesdale, PA, ca. 1892-1923.

J. D. Bergen Co.

Meriden, CT, ca. 1880-1922. Marks left to right: paper label only, shield and script acid stamp only.

Etched.

Paper label only.   Etched.

Buffalo Cut Glass

Buffalo, NY, ca.1902-1918. This mark appeared as a paper label only and was never used as an acid stamp.

Paper label only.

C.F.Monroe

Meriden, CT, ca. 1903-1916. C.F.M. Co. is a rare cut glass mark identified by the lower case letter "o" in Co. The authentic C.F.M.CO. with an upper case letter "O" in CO. is stamped in metal only; it should not be found on cut glass. The elaborate mongram appeared as a trademark in advertising, stationery, etc.; it was never used as a mark.

C.F.M.Co.
On cut glass.

C.F.M.CO.
Stamped in metal only.

Used as trademark only, never as a mark on glass.

T.B. Clark Co.

Honesdale, PA, ca. 1884-1930. Lines in the bottle mark should be reasonably clear and open. Forgeries of that mark tend to be filled in and blurred. Original Clark script marks may appear with or without the words Trade Mark. The position of Trade Mark may also show slight variations. Typical acid forgeries of the script marks are filled and blurred. The name Clark also appears in all upper case letters. Original letter style is a Roman or serif face; many forgeries of this mark are in a block or sans serif style.

Original Clark marks

Crosshatching in original bottle is reasonably open.

Original Clark script mark may or may not include the words Trade Mark.

CLARK
Original mark in serif styled letters.

Clark maple leaf. Also see Maple City mark, page 82.

Typical Clark forgeries

CLARK
Forgeries often appear as block-style lettering; usually blurred.

Bottle-mark forgeries are usually blurred with bottle filled-in.

Typical script forgery.

73

Pope Cut Glass

New York, NY, ca. 1916-mid-1920s. DiamonKut was a trade name for a particular line of cut glass.

Paper label only.

Dorflinger & Sons

White Mills, PA, ca. 1865-1921. Colored and cut glass, ca. 1865-1921. This trademark was used as a paper label only; it was never acid etched or engraved.

Two acid-stamped forgeries are known; decanter mark, left; fantasy forgery, right.

Egginton Rich Cut Glass Co.,

Corning, NY, ca. 1899-1920.

Empire Cut Glass Co.

Flemington, NJ, ca. 1895 1925, paper label only.

Paper label only.

Fry Glass Co.

Makers of cut glass and art glass, ca. 1901-1933.

Genuine small acid-etched script mark, about three-sixteenths of an inch tall.

Genuine script in shield, under three-eighths inch tall.

FRY Co.

Forged acid-etched block-letter fantasy mark. No old counterpart.

Fantasy acid-etched script mark.

Forged acid-etched script mark with large fat letters, over one-quarter inch tall. Often smudged with ragged edged appearance.

Design Guild
Sandblasted mark found on colored overlay new cut glass with realistic patterns. Country of origin unknown.

The Design Guild mark, upper right, is found on this green overlay cut to clear 10-inch bowl. Detailed scene of barnyard with rooster, hens and chicks.

Cut Glass

T.G. Hawkes & Co.

Corning, NY, ca. 1880-1962.

The Hawkes firm was one of the largest producers of American Brilliant Period cut glass. At the turn of the 19th century, Libbey Glass was Hawkes' nearest rival in cut glass volume. Many of Hawkes blanks were made at the Steuben Glass Works also located in Corning, NY. Over 322 patterns of stemware alone were in production during the company's peak years. When business declined, Hawkes sold its molds and patterns to the United States Glass Co. in Tiffin, Ohio. Hawkes cut glass closed in 1962.

Authentic Hawkes marks

Ca. 1890-1905.

Ca. 1905-1920 on intaglio engraved glass.

Primarily ca. 1905-1940, then limited use to 1962.

HAWKES

Ca. 1910-1962, primarily on stemware.

Hawkes Hunter, Waher, 1984

Genuine block-style mark on the top side of a stemware foot.

Genuine 1890-1905 acid-stamped mark on the bottom of a stopper. Actual size of mark is less than three-eighths inch tall.

76

Typical forgeries of Hawkes marks

Hawkes Hunter,
Waher, 1984

Forged "Hawkes" mark in script applied with a diamond-tip pen. All original Hawkes marks were applied with an acid stamp, not engraved.

Typical Hawkes acid- stamped forgeries generally appear partially filled in and blurred. Many fake marks are quite large, one-half inch and taller.

GRAVIC

Fantasy mark added above genuine old marks, as well as appearing by itself.

HAWKS

Misspelled with no "E." Found on various pieces of new stemware.

L. Hinsberger & Bro.
New York, NY, ca. 1895-1913.
Paper label only, never acid-stamped.

Hope Glass Works
Providence, RI, ca. 1873-1925.
A few family members working as individuals used the company name until ca. 1950.

Cut Glass

J. Hoare & Co.

Corning, NY, ca. 1853-1920.

The 1853 in the center of the mark on left refers to the year the company started. This mark was not used on cut glass until 1895.

Honesdale Decorating Co.

Honesdale, PA, ca. 1901-1932.

The company was started by C. Dorflinger & Sons glass of White Mills, PA, as a decorating shop. From the beginning, the Honesdale operation was run by Carl Prosch, a glass designer decorator. Prosch bought the Honesdale operation in 1916 and continued the business until 1932.

HDC monogram superimposed over a goblet was used as a paper label only.

Script mark always in gold, never used as an acid stamp.

Registered trademark of Honesdale Decorating Company, the HDC monogram over a goblet. This trademark was used in legal documents, stationery, etc., not as a mark on glass.

78

Hunt Glass

Corning, NY, ca. 1895-1935. Some family members continued small scale production until 1973.

Acid-stamp mark, ca. 1906-1915.   Paper label only.

Imperial Glass Co.

NUCUT is a molded mark used on pressed glass imitations of cut glass introduced ca. 1910. The mark usually appears on the inside bottom surface, not on the outside bottom (also see the main Imperial Glass listing in the Pressed Glass chapter).

Iorio Glass Shop

Flemington, NJ, ca. 1950 by glass cutter and designer Louis Orio, formerly of Empire Cut Glass.

Irving Glass Co.

Honesdale, PA, ca. 1900-1933.

Cut Glass

Libbey Glass Co.

Toledo, OH, ca. 1892-present.

The Libbey mark with eagle and Libbey Cut Glass has never been documented as a permanent mark on any authentic Libbey cut glass. The only use of the eagle mark on cut glass was a paper label, not an acid mark. The eagle mark has only been found in red on white opaque glass, mostly souvenirs sold at Libbey's pavilion at the 1892 Columbian World's Fair. Any acid-etched eagle mark should be highly suspect.

Libbey and Hawkes, were the largest volume producers of cut glass. All-over cutting on thick, heavy blanks was gradually discontinued after WW I. Libbey continued to make at least some hand-cut pieces up until about 1940. (also see Libbey entries in Art Glass and Pressed Glass sections).

Authentic Libbey marks on cut glass products

Ca. 1892-1896
Used on cut glass as paper label only, not an acid stamp.

Ca. 1896-1906
First acid stamp mark on heavy cut glass.

Ca. 1906-WW I era
Acid stamp mark on cut glass.

Ca. 1919-1930
Acid stamp mark used after ca. WW I up through the 1930s. This mark would not appear on brilliant period cut glass.

Officially listed by Libbey as a ca. 1939-1945 trademark. However, there is little practical difference between this and the 1919-1930 acid mark.

Ca. 1900-1910

Paper label only, white letters on blue. The hole in the middle of the label was placed over acid stamps on cut glass to help retail customers find the Libbey trademark. Used early 1900s. Logically, this label should only be found on or at least near an acid mark. This label was promoted in various advertisements of the period.

ca. mid-1930s

Usually a paper label, a few examples have been found acid-stamped on Libbey-Nash series, ca. mid-1930s.

ca. 1901-1930s

Found on pressed glass blanks, not blown blanks, ca. 1901-1930s. (Also see Straus & Sons mark.)

Common Libbey forgeries on cut glass

The Libbey sword, the earliest original acid mark, is frequently forged. Typical examples like this one show blurring and normally open areas filled-in with acid.

The "Libbey Cut Glass" mark is often applied as an acid stamp. This mark was only used on cut glass as a paper label, never an acid stamp.

Rubber stamps in simple block letters, the kind you can order through office supply stores, are frequently used to apply forged acid marks.

Lotus Cut Glass Co

Barnesville, OH, ca. 1911. Paper label only; still in the gift business in the mid-1990s.

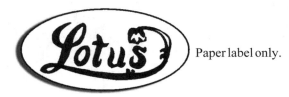

Paper label only.

Cut Glass

Maple City Glass Co.

Honesdale, PA, ca. 1900-1912.

These two leaf marks were used only by Maple City. A third leaf mark is virtually identical to a leaf mark also used by T.B. Clark Cut Glass which bought Maple City (also see T.B. Clark in this chapter).

These leaf marks were used by Maple City Glass Co. only, ca. 1900-1912.

This leaf mark was used by both Maple City Glass Co. and T.B. Clark Cut Glass which eventually bought Maple City. This mark could appear on glass made ca. 1900-1930.

Meriden Cut Glass Co.

Meriden, CT, ca. 1876-1896. Originally applied as a paper label only, never an acid stamp.

Paper label only.

Mt. Washington Glass Co.

Mt. Washington cut glass was not permanently marked. The only authentic factory-applied identification was one of two paper labels shown below; neither mark was ever used as an acid stamp. Modern forgers have converted the art work from both of these marks into rubber stamps to apply acid.

Paper labels only, not acid-stamped. Left, Russian Crystal; right, Trademark Mt. W.G. Co.

F.X. Parsche

Chicago, IL, ca 1876-1917. Family descendants Donald and Russ Parsche were still cutting glass through the 1980s.

Pitkin & Brooks

Chicago, IL, ca 1872-1920.

Cambridge Glass Co.

Cambridge, OH. The mark NEARCUT is molded in pressed glass that imitates cut glass. It never appeared as an acid etched or engraved mark.

Pairpoint Corp

New Bedford, MA, 1900-1938. Pairpoint Corp. never marked any cut glass with an acid stamp. Any Pairpoint acid-stamped mark, like the three shown below, is a forgery (also see Pairpoint listing in Art Glass chapter).

Acid-etched Pairpoint forgeries.

All acid etched Pairpoint marks are fake. Many of these fake marks are copied from trademarks that appear in reference books. The most common are the three shown above. The P in diamond and script Pairpoint are authentic marks but never used as acid marks. Pairpoint Mfg. Co. is a fantasy mark; the closest original counterpart is The Pairpoint Corp'n, used only on reverse painted lamp shades and applied in ink.

McKee-Jeanette Glass Works

Jeanette, PA. PRESCUT is a molded mark on pressed glass imitations of cut glass made, ca. 1910-1930s. The mark is usually found on the inside bottoms of bowls and dishes.

Cut Glass

Paper label only.

Cut Glass Corp of America

Also known as Quaker City Cut Glass Co., Philadelphia, PA, 1904-1927. Paper label only; no acid-stamped mark has ever been authenticated.

H. P. Sinclaire & Co.

Corning, NY, ca. 1904-1929.

There are two shields in the wreath; a fleur-de-lis is in the left shield, a thistle in the right. The authentic acid stamp is very small, about one-quarter-inch across. Most fakes are quite large.

Sterling Glass Co

Cincinnati, OH, ca. 1902-1950.

Paper label only.

Straus & Sons

New York, NY. Started ca. 1888, still in business during the 1990s as Straus-Duparquet. The Straus Cut Glass with gemstone was used as a paper label only, never an acid mark. The star in circle was acid stamped on fully cut pieces (a similar mark by Libbey appears on pressed blanks).

Etched.

Stuart & Sons LTD

Stourbridge, England, since mid-19th century, still in business. Primarily fine stemware but also custom work and decorative pieces. Virtually all pieces are marked with the etched trademark shown here. Sometimes the word England will appear with the mark.

One of the forged marks in circulation has quote marks around Stuart.

Tuthill Cut Glass

Middletown, NY, ca. 1900-1923. Actual size of genuine mark is very small, only about one-half inch wide. Most forgeries are quite large, one-inch or more.

Unger Brothers,
Newark, NJ, ca. 1901-1918.

Acid stamped.

Paper label only.

Thomas Webb & Sons
See listing under Art Glass.

Webb-Corbett
See listing under Art Glass.

Pressed Glass

Glass is fragile. Almost everyone knows that because we've seen firsthand what happens when glass is dropped. Yet the molds in which pressed glass is made can last almost indefinitely.

Many molds of the L. G. Wright Glass Company auctioned in 1999, for example, dated back to the 1930s; some reportedly from the 19th century. Molds from failed glass companies like Cambridge, Imperial, Westmoreland, Heisey and others, continue in production today, decades after their original owners left the glass business forever.

Collectors need to face the fact that many molds never die; they just fade into production at another glass factory. One of the ways to date these pieces is to know and understand which company added what marks to which molds during what years.

This chapter lists marks on American pressed glass over the last 20 years, as well as their genuinely old counterparts if any exist.

Some reproductions made from new molds, like this Grape Delight nut dish in carnival, have new marks added. This piece has the letter N in a circle, a mark copied from an old Northwood mark.

Other reproductions are made from original molds. This Bashful Charlotte flower figure was first made by Cambridge. Yet decades after Cambridge closed, the mold was back in production.

Simulated molded, or embossed, lettering on a new bottle, "Dr. Chervenka's Skunk River Bicycle Tonic, Clive, Iowa." Bottle is aqua glass, square shaped body with pouring spout. Made by a California firm which offers custom lettering on glass.

New

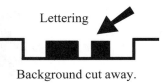

Lettering

Background cut away.

New designs and lettering are created by removing the surface from the background. The exact method varies but the result is always the same–a roughened or substantially different finish on the background surrounding the letters or design. Sharp lines are the result of some mechanical operation performed after the glass has cooled.

Old

Lettering

Lettering above background.

Molded, or embossed, lettering and designs on all genuinely old bottles are almost always raised above the surrounding surface. Edges on molded letters and designs are generally rounded or sloped. Molded glass cannot be formed into precisely sharp straight lines because 1) it sags in the mold, and 2) it would not easily be released from the mold.

Pressed Glass

Stencils and masks used in forming new letters by sandblasting and acid etching frequently leave clues. Gaps in the stencils and masks frequently have gaps or tears which allow the abrasive or acid to leak through. A gap at the corner of the mask used to create the new letters shown here left a permanent line where the acid or abrasive attacked the glass (arrow).

AB–Botson Glass Co.
Molded AB monogram mark used from ca. 1980 on.

AHRC–American Historical Replica Co.
Molded mark on historical pattern glass reissues.

B–in circle
Mark of Edna Barnes. Barnes designed various glass products, especially glass reamers. She jobbed production from her private molds to various glass houses, ca 1980s.

B–in diamond

Molded raised B in molded raised diamond is the mark of Boyd's Crystal Art Glass, Inc. The company was started in 1978 after buying out Degenhart Glass (Crystal Art Glass Co.). Boyd controls over 200 molds, mostly small items such as salts, toothpick holders, animal figurines and similar pieces.

Boyd has consistently marked its products with the molded B inside a diamond. On most products, a bar has been added for every five years of production, dating pieces in five-year periods. Although this system is generally accurate, it is not absolute.

Boyd products are periodically reissued in slightly different colors. The company claims to have over 300 different colors.

| 1978-1983 | 1983-1988 | 1988-1993 | 1993-1998 | 1998-2003 |

Boyd's Crystal Art Glass marks are divided into five-year production periods. Every five years, a bar is added to the basic B inside diamond raised molded mark.

Photo of Boyd's Crystal Art Glass molded mark. The arrangement of lines date the production period as 1993-1998. In actual practice, the date lines may or may not touch.

Pressed Glass

B– in triangle

Guernsey Glass, ca. 1980s, including toothpicks, salts, novelties, limited editions, etc. Molded dates will sometimes be included with marks but the dates have nothing to do with year of production. Pieces marked 1981, for example, were in production throughout the 1990s and into 2000.

Basic molded B in triangle
mark of Guernsey Glass.

Some marks include dates.
However, the dates don't
always correspond to the
actual date of production.

This egg cup with child's
face is a Guersey Glass
product in a Victorian style.

Bee (insect)

Bryce Higbee & Co. was established by John Bryce in 1879. One of the company marks, ca. 1900-1920, was a bee molded in the glass with the letter H on the left wing, the letter I on the body and the letter

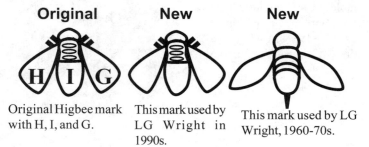

Original

New

New

Original Higbee mark
with H, I, and G.

This mark used by
LG Wright in
1990s.

This mark used by LG
Wright, 1960-70s.

G on the right wing. This mark has been copied by modern glass companies including L.G. Wright and Mosser. The original and Wright copies are shown here; the Mosser versions are shown under the Mosser Glass listing in this section.

John Bull–on eyecup

New pressed glass eyecups produced in the 1990s were marked almost the same as vintage pieces. Both new and old, shown below, included the patent date of 1917. The important difference separating new from old is "Made in USA," which appears on the old (arrow) but not the new. Marks appear on the bottom of the base.

New John Bull eyecup, left, does not include Made in USA. Old John Bull eyecup has Made in USA in center.

C–in hexagon

The raised molded letter C in a raised molded hexagon is the mark of J & B Glass Co., ca.1980s. Glass novelties, limited editions.

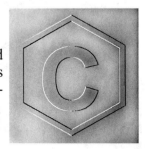

C–in triangle, etched

Acid etched or sandblasted C inside a triangle. Applied with a stencil, which leaves gaps in the triangle. Cambridge Glass Co., Cambridge, OH. This is an authentic mark originally used on laboratory glass only. Found forged on reproduction flower holders and other colored glass in the 1990s.

Pressed Glass

C–in triangle, molded

Raised molded C inside a raised molded triangle was originally used by Cambridge Glass Co., Cambridge, OH, ca. 1920-1954.

Some reproductions of Cambridge Caprice made from original molds are marked with a small raised dot of glass. Not all new pieces have the dot. Some dots have been removed by secondary sellers.

New Caprice covered butter dish made from old mold. Some, but not all, new Caprice butter dishes are marked with a raised dot of glass in the top side of the base (arrow). Made by an American glass factory.

New blue look-alike Caprice sugar bowl. Marked JAPAN on bottom rim in molded letters.

CB–Clevenger Bros
Clevenger Bros Glass Works
Clevenger Glass

Three brothers–Tom, Reno and Allie Clevenger– started a glass house in 1930 that specialized in reproductions of early American glass in the South Jersey style. The company was operated under the name Clevenger Brothers Glass Company until 1966 when the business came under control of James Travis, who changed the name to Clevenger Brothers Glass Works.

While early Clevenger free-blown pieces are collectible in their own right, many Clevenger pieces are incorrectly identified. This is a fairly easy mistake since most of its work up until 1980 has pontil marks which collectors immediately assume indicates an early piece. Clevenger's Jenny Lind and EG Booz bottles are particularly confusing.

Early pieces up until 1955 are rarely marked. Between 1955 and 1966, some pieces were marked with embossed raised letters CB. Most, but far from all, Clevenger pieces made under Travis since 1966 have a large CB in the base. The letters may appear side-by-side or one either side of the pontil. Some pieces are further marked with the full name of the company, Clevenger Brothers Glassworks, which is often abbreviated in several different ways depending on space.

Large CB used after 1966. Letters are about one-half inch tall. Marks usually appear in base.

Post-1966 example of the full name spelled out, Clevenger Bros Glass Wks. Before 1966, the name was Clevenger Brothers Glass Company.

93

Pressed Glass

Group of Clevenger Brothers Glass Works reproductions from a 1990s catalog page.

D–D in heart

Raised molded D is the trademark of Crystal Art Glass Co. This company, owned by J and E Degenhart, is commonly called Degenhart Glass by collectors rather than the more formal name, Crystal Art Glass.

The company operated from 1947 until 1978, when the works was purchased by the Boyd family to form Boyd's Crystal Art Glass, Inc. The D alone and D inside the heart were used ca. 1947 to 1978. In 1978, Island Mold Co. removed the D from some molds.

Some pre-1978 stock with the letter D was still available at the Degenhart museum through the 1980s and 1990s.

1947-1978   1947-1978   after 1978

Duboe

Duboe is the name of a company that appears on a glass hand-held reamer along with a patent date. There are two reproductions of this reamer. One from Taiwan does not have the Duboe mark. A second reproduction made in America does have the Duboe patent mark. Both reproductions have been in the market since the early

94

1990s. Both styles of reproductions have been made in clear, as well as colors.

Original Duboe hand-held reamers were made in clear colorless glass only. Any colored version is a reproduction. You can also separate old from new by examining the top rim. Both the Taiwanese and American reproductions have a molded texture in the rim. The rim on an original hand-held Duboe is perfectly smooth without any molded texture.

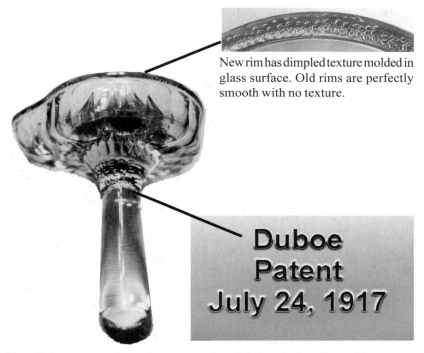

New rim has dimpled texture molded in glass surface. Old rims are perfectly smooth with no texture.

New Duboe reamers have the same mark molded on the handle as old reamers.

E & E

The raised molded mark E & E is the mark of E & E Collectables which bought out the molds of Wetzel Glass. It jobbed out the molds to various glass houses to produce salts, novelties, etc. around 1986.

Pressed Glass

Easley

The molded Easley name and an 1888 patent date appear on both old and reproduction pressed glass reamers. So far, all reproductions have been made in colored glass. Originals were made only in clear colorless glass.

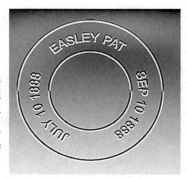

Both new and old reamers have the company name and 1888 patent date molded in the base.

New and old pressed glass reamers marked Easley with an 1888 patent date. So far, new reamers, left, have been made in various colors. Originals, right, were made in clear colorless glass only.

Fenton

Fenton Glass was founded in 1907. In 1974, the company trademark, the word Fenton in script placed inside an oval, began to be molded into glassware. Fenton began dating its marks with a single digit to indicate the decade of production in 1980. The first decade mark was 8 for the 1980s, 9 for the 1990s and so on.

Fenton marks are usually very clear on pressed wares. Marks can be very blurred or almost nonexistent on blown-molded pieces. On blown pieces, the mark is originally placed on the gather in the spot or pattern mold. Blowing out the glass frequently distorts or flattens the mark.

Basic raised molded script Fenton mark in pressed glass since 1974.

Beginning in 1980, a single digit representing the decade of production was added to the molded mark. An eight designates the 1980s.

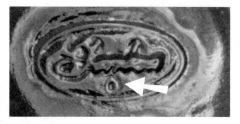

Fenton marks in blown-molded wares are often blurred. This mark is from the bottom of a blown-molded pickle castor insert. Note the decade digit 0, indicating production in the first decade of the 21st century.

The original 1950s Fenton Chickenserver was not marked. Fenton made the piece again in 1996 when it was marked with the Fenton oval and 9 to indicate the decade of production, 1990s. It was made a third time for Martha Stewart in 1999. Pieces made for Stewart are marked in the lid only with a very small Fenton oval and 9. The Stewart version is shown here.

Pressed Glass

Fenton and star

The stand raised molded Fenton oval and a raised molded star appear on products Fenton made for Kaleidoscope Inc., ca. 1980s. The Fenton mark does not have the decade digit. The star and Fenton mark can appear in widely separate places; they are not necessarily placed together.

G–in star

Raised molded G inside raised molded star is the mark of Gaskills Glass. This firm did not make any glass but jobbed out work to various glass houses. Products included small novelty pieces, limited edition figures, etc., ca. 1980s.

Gillinder Glass

The name Gillinder has been associated with American Glass since 1861. The business has been known under various names throughout the years: Franklin Flint Glass Co., 1861; Gillinder & Bennett, 1863; Gillinder & Sons, 1867; Gillinder Bros. Inc., from 1923. During the 1990s, the general trade name was simply Gillinder Glass.

Very few pre-1990 pieces were permanently marked. The major exceptions were small pieces produced at the factory's on-site glass works at the 1876 Centennial in Philadelphia. On some, but not all, pieces made at the time of the Centennial and a short time afterwards, Gillinder & Sons appears in molded lettering. On some pieces, the molded words, Centennial Exhibition, also appear.

Most pieces made during the first half of the 20th century were not marked. Through ca. 1960 to 1980, many pieces were marked with a paper label reading Gillinder Since 1861. This label was not permanent and easily removed.

In about 1990, but not before, a new molded mark was used on some reissues from genuinely old molds. This mark includes the word Gillinder in script above the word Glass in block letters. Among the new pieces reissued from old molds that have the new mark are a pug dog figurine and peacock vase.

Molded mark on some 19th century pieces. May include the additional words, Centennial Exhibition.

Paper label only, used ca. 1960-1980s.

Raised molded mark that appears on some, but not all, new Gillinder Glass from about 1990, but not before then.

H–bisected

Molded H is the mark of Vi Hunter, a glass designer of the 1980s. Actual production jobbed out to various manufacturers. Includes figurines, cup plates, novelty items.

H–in diamond

The molded H–in diamond was the original trademark of A. H. Heisey, ca. 1893-1984, of Newark, OH. The original mark is distinctly shaped as a vertical diamond. Squat, square molded copies of the H in diamond have appeared on reproductions sold by American reproduction wholesalers since the 1980s.

So far, no fake mark has appeared on copies of original Heisey

Pressed Glass

shapes. The fake marks have appeared only on fantasy shapes, pieces and patterns never made by Heisey.

Fake
Heisey mark.

Original
Heisey mark.

Federal Glass

Federal Glass was founded about 1900 as a bottle and jar manufacturer. Production later switched to tumblers, stemware and tableware in the 1920s-1930s-1940s. Ovenware was also included. The firm was declared bankrupt in 1980.

The raised molded mark of the letter F in a shield appears on some, but far from all, products. Inexperienced sellers, particularly on Internet auction sites, will occasionally mistake and list this mark as Fenton.

HA

A raised molded HA is a mark used by Hazel-Atlas Glass Co. The company began as Hazel Glass in 1886. In 1902, it merged with the Atlas Glass Co. to become Hazel-Atlas. At its height, the company was producing glass in 14 different plants across America.

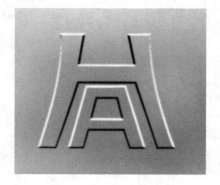

The products of Hazel-Atlas are of particular interest to collectors of Depression-era glasswares. Although the molded mark does not appear on most tablewares, it is commonly found on storage jars, bottles, ovenware and tumblers.

Several patterns and pieces of glass originally made by Hazel-Atlas during the 1920s-1940s has been reproduced. Among these is a close copy of a two-cup measure with reamer. You can separate old from new by looking at the markings on the bottoms of the cups.

Original Hazel-Atlas glass two-cup measure with reamer lid, right. Reproduction, left, is virtually identical except for markings on the bottoms.

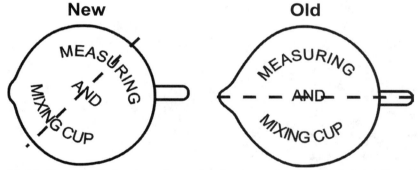

Molded lettering in bottom of reproduction two-cup measure, left, is aligned at about a 45-degree angle to the spout and handle. Molded lettering in the original, right, is aligned parallel to the spout and handle.

HFM

The raised molded letters HFM appear on pressed glass historical reproductions sold through the Henry Ford Museum in the 1960s. These pieces were made for the museum by Fostoria.

Pressed Glass

IG–Imperial

Imperial Glass Corp. began production in 1903. It was an independent operation until 1973. It was purchased in 1973 by Lenox, Inc., which operated it as a Lenox subsidiary until 1981. Lenox sold the operation to investor Arthur Lynch in 1981 and by 1982 the company was forced into bankruptcy. The final owner was Robert Stahl, who presided over the last days of the firm which closed for good in 1984. The main factory buildings were demolished in 1995.

Many marks were used over the years; some permanently molded in the glass, others only used as labels or in advertising. In the last years, as ownership frequently changed, marks become confused and vary considerably.

Cross mark, molded only, ca. 1914-1930s.

A number of molds with various Imperial Corp. marks originally used 1951-1984 are still in existence. These molds have been sporadically put back in produc-

IG mark, #1, originally used ca. 1951-73. Lenox Inc. buys Imperial in 1973 and adds letter L to IG, mark #2, ca. 1973-81. Lenox Inc., sells Imperial to Arthur Lorch, who adds letter A to LIG, mark #3, ca. 1981-84. A few pieces made 1982-84 are marked NI for New Imperial, mark #4.

Photo of Imperial mark #3, ca. 1981-84. Includes the original IG for Imperial Glass, L for Lenox and A for Arthur Lorch. Shown as it appears on a new piece of vaseline glass.

tion by various contemporary glass makers. New glass made in those molds has the 1951-1984 molded marks.

Imperial also bought many of the molds of Cambridge Glass when that company closed in 1954. Imperial modified a number of the Cambridge molds for its own use. In 1981, for example, Imperial used a modified Cambridge mold to produce the six and one-half inch Bashful Charlotte flower figure for a marketing firm by the name of Mirror Images (MI). MI sold the Charlotte figures under the name Venus Rising. Although some MI pieces were marked MI only (see MI listing in this chapter), Venus Rising was marked IG and 81 on the base. Large quantities of these pieces were still being wholesaled as recently as 1995.

For other Imperial marks, see NuArt and NuCut in this same chapter.

The six-and-one half-inch Bashful Charlotte from a modified Cambridge mold as it was marketed by Mirror Images.

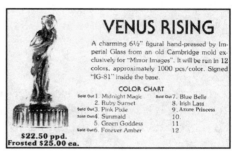

VENUS RISING

A charming 6½" figural hand-pressed by Imperial Glass from an old Cambridge mold exclusively for "Mirror Images". It will be run in 12 colors, approximately 1000 pcs/color. Signed "IG-81" inside the base.

COLOR CHART

Sold Out 1. Midnight Magic	Sold Out 7. Blue Belle
2. Ruby Sunset	8. Irish Lass
Sold Out 3. Pink Pixie	9. Azure Princess
Sold Out 4. Sunmaid	10.
5. Green Goddess	11.
Sold Out 6. Forever Amber	12.

$22.50 ppd.
Frosted $25.00 ea.

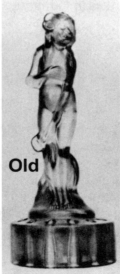

New　　**Old**

Venus Rising by Imperial, left. Original six-and-one-half-inch Bashful Charlotte, right. Note that the modified mold includes vertical ribs around the base. The original base is smooth-sided.

Pressed Glass

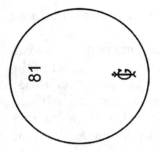

The Venus Rising figure was marked IG and 81 up under the base. Since the 81 and IG are so far apart, the 81 is frequently not recognized as a date.

IG

A mark similar to Imperial Glass, this IG was used by Iroquois Glass Industries of Canada, 1958-1967. The Canadian mark appears mostly on bottles and other glass containers.

IGCO

Another mark often confused with Imperial's IG is this mark of Illinois Glass Co. This mark has been used since 1914 on glass bottles and jars. It is formed of the large letters IG, with smaller letters of CO across middle. The O is filled in and appears as a solid disc.

K–KW

The molded letter K, alone or with the letter W, is the mark of John Kemple Glassworks. Kemple operated from ca. 1945 until about 1971, when the founder John died.

In 1971, Wheaton Glass Co., a division of Wheaton Industries owned by Frank Wheaton, Jr., bought many of the Kemple molds. Wheaton put the molds into production for his Wheatonware division which sold glass through a home-party plan similar to Tupperware.

Early Wheatonware production carried the same mark, if any, as the Kemple pieces. Later, the letter W was added to many molds to distinguish pieces made in them from original Kemple pieces.

The Kemple molds were signed over to Wheaton Village in 1975. Wheaton Village of Milville, NJ, is an historical preservation association dedicated to the preservation and showcasing of American crafts, especially glass.

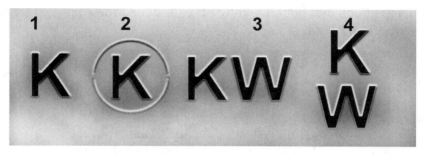

Marks of John Kemple Glassworks, ca. 1945-1971, are the letter K, mark #1; the letter K inside a circle, mark #2. Glass made from Kemple molds after they were obtained by Wheaton Glass and Wheaton Village in 1971 were marked with the letters K and W. The letter W either followed the K, as in mark #3, or appeared below the K, as in mark #4.

L–L in circle

The molded script letter L, by itself or inside a circle, is a mark of Libbey Glass. This mark appears on pressed glass for institutional and home use, primarily tumblers and bar ware. It was registered in 1937 but wasn't in widespread use until after WW II, ca. 1946. It continues to be used through the present day. Whether the L appears alone or inside the circle does not determine age; the marks are used interchangeably. Both marks are almost always placed in the outside bottoms of pieces. Marks are quite small, both about one-quarter inch tall.

Pressed Glass

McKee

New milk glass with the molded McKee script mark first started appearing in 1998. The new McKee script mark ends in a rounded curve. The original script McKee mark hooks backwards.

All the new pieces marked McKee are made by Summit Glass. Since none of the McKee items are listed in Summit's general price list, it's assumed, but not known for sure, that the McKee pieces are private mold work.

New raised molded "McKee" script mark on reproductions. Note that leg of the letter K ends in large semicircular curve. The legs of the M are of equal length.

Original raised molded McKee script mark. Note how the leg of the letter K loops backwards. The first leg of the letter M is longer than the other leg.

The new McKee molded mark appears on two types of base. One is the classic split rib McKee base, shown here, which will accept genuinely old McKee lids. Other bases with the new McKee mark fit only the matching lid and were not originally made by McKee.

MMA–Metropolitan Museum of Art

Raised molded letters in pressed glass reproductions sold by the MMA gift shop and catalog.

M–M in circle–M in outline of Ohio

These are molded marks of Mosser Glass. Mosser Glass has specialized in reproductions of antique glass since 1971. Many of its products are made from original molds. Other pieces are made from new molds that imitate old patterns.

Marks of Mosser Glass include the letter M in a circle, the letter M alone and the letter M inside the outline of the state of Ohio.

Combination of Higbee Glass mark and Mosser Glass Company mark on ABC plate. Mosser bought the original Higbee ABC plate mold and added the Mosser mark next to the original Higbee bee mark. (see Higbee Glass this section).

Selection of new inverted thistle pressed glass offered by Mosser Glass. From a 2001 catalog page.

Pressed Glass

Martha Stewart

Many of the glass items sold through Martha by Mail, a mail order catalog of Martha Stewart, are reproductions of antique shapes. Some of the new glass is marked Martha by Mail in raised glass. Both Fenton and LE Smith glass companies make glass for Stewart.

New 10- inch cake stand, left, is marked Martha by Mail in small molded raised glass letters along bottom rim, right.

MI

The molded letters MI were used by Mirror Images, a Michigan base marketing firm. This company sponsored reissues and reproduction glass figures made from original Heisey, Imperial, Cambridge and New Martinsville molds. The new production was handled by Imperial Glass and Viking Glass.

Some of the figures MI commissioned were two figural flower holders originally made by Cambridge. When Cambridge closed, the molds for most of the flower figures were bought by Imperial Glass. Imperial modified two molds for Mirror Image: the six-and-one-half

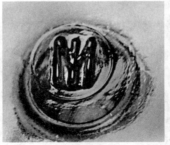

Raised molded mark of Mirror Images is a monogram formed of the letters MI. Close up photo, left; illustration, right.

inch Bashful Charlotte and the eight-and-one-half-inch Draped Lady.

In 1985, Imperial made the eight-and one-half-inch Draped Lady, shown here, for MI. This piece was marked MI in raised molded letters. The mark is way up under the bottom of the base and is difficult to see.

In 1981, Imperial produced the six-and one-half-inch Bashful Charlotte, which Mirror Image sold as "Venus Rising." This piece was not marked MI, but was marked IG (see Imperial Glass listing in this chapter).

Not all of the MI products are known. Previously unknown products continue to show up. A pair of amber perfume bottles, for example, recently showed up at a Midwest auction. Since all of the MI pieces were made from vintage molds of various glass companies, MI pieces can easily be confused with those of the vintage makers.

Amber perfume marked MI on base.

Modified Draped Lady, left, as it was modified by Imperial for Mirror Images (MI) in 1985. The new flower holder is marked MI.

Pressed Glass

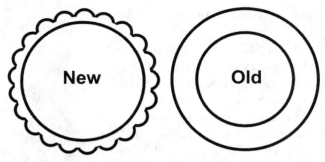

View of bases of the 8½-inch Imperial Draped Lady, left, and the original 8½-inch Cambridge Draped Lady, right. When the Cambridge flower figures were modified, ridges were added around the base. Walls of the modified bases were also made much thinner than the walls of old bases.

N–N in circle

The original molded mark with the letter N in a circle is the mark of the Northwood Glass Co. in production ca. 1880-1923. All authentic Northwood marks with the letter N include a circle, no exceptions. Some circles may be faint, but there is always a circle with

Original N in circle mark has a perfectly formed circle and a bar under the N.

Imitation does not include bar below N. Found on Italian reproductions from the 1980s.

Imitation missing both bar below N and circle. Appeared mid-1980s, source unknown.

Two marks of L.G. Wright. An extra leg added, left, the N almost touching the circle, right.

genuine marks (#1).

There are many imitations and look-alike marks to the original N in circle. Some are missing the bar below the N (#2), others do not include a circle (#3). Many are simply poorly formed with sections of the circle or N incomplete. In a new example from Mosser Glass, for instance, the left half of the circle is completely missing.

With some marks, it's not what's missing, but what's added like the L.G. Wright marks. The story goes that Wright bought some original Northwood molds with original marks. When he took the molds to Fenton for production, Fenton refused unless the Northwood mark was removed or altered. Wright compromised by adding a diagonal "leg" to the left of the original N (#4).

In another Wright look-alike Northwood mark, the N almost touches the circle (#5). Original marks have the N perfectly centered in the circle. Although Wright is out of business, its confusing marks will be with collectors for years to come. Many of Wright's molds liquidated at auction in 1999 were purchased by two American reproduction wholesalers. A number of those molds were back in production by 2001 with the Wright marks (also see Wright listing later in this same section).

Some of the more confusing shapes with imitation N marks are tumblers made in carnival and custard. A quick way to separate old from new is this simple guideline: All old Northwood tumblers are marked on the inside bottom. If you find a Northwood mark on the outside bottom, the mark is automatically a fake.

This imitation N in circle mark, left, is on this reproduction Grape Delight pattern nut bowl, right, made by Mosser Glass beginning in the late 1970s. Note that the left side of the circle is incomplete. Circles around the N in authentic marks are perfectly formed. The original Grape Delight nut bowl was made by Dugan, not Northwood.

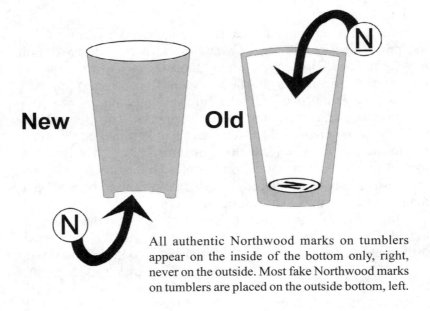

New

Old

All authentic Northwood marks on tumblers appear on the inside of the bottom only, right, never on the outside. Most fake Northwood marks on tumblers are placed on the outside bottom, left.

NEARCUT

Cambridge Glass Co., Cambridge, OH. Used on pressed blown glass that imitated cut glass. The mark is molded in raised letters. It never appeared as an acid etched or engraved mark (also see Cambridge entry in this same chapter).

NEARCUT

Northwood

A raised molded facsimile signature. This mark appears on original custard in Nautilus and Chrysanthemum Sprig and opalescent pieces.

Opalescent town pumps, copied from a Northwood original, have been reproduced for years. Only original opalescent pumps have the molded Northwood script mark, the reproductions do not have the script mark.

(For Northwood marks with the letter N, look under N in this same section).

NuArt–NuCut

Both NuArt and NuCut are molded marks used by the original Imperial Glass company of Bellaire, OH. NuCut was molded on Imperial's pressed glass, ca. 1914-1930s, made to resemble cut glass. This mark appeared only as a molded mark; it was never acid stamped or engraved.

NuArt was a similar mark which appeared on pressed gas and electric shades. This mark also appeared as a raised molded mark only; it was never acid stamped or engraved.

Forged acid stamped NuArt marks have appeared on a wide variety of glass shades, especially old but originally unmarked shades with two and one-quarter inch fitter rims. Forged NuArt marks have also been found on new and old art glass. NuArt was only used to mark shades, never art or decorative glass.

NuCut was a molded mark only that appeared on pressed glass imitations of cut glass, ca. 1914-1930s.

NuArt was a molded mark used only on pressed glass gas and electric shades.

Forged acid-stamped NuArt marks frequently show up on glass shades with 2¼-inch fitter rims. Authentic NuArt marks are molded only, never acid stamped.

OSV

The raised molded letters OSV for the mark of Old Sturbridge Village Museum Shop. This mark appears on replicas and reproductions sold in the museum's gift shop and catalog.

Pressed Glass

P–in diamond

The molded P in a diamond is a trademark of Pairpoint Glass. This mark, however, was never permanently applied to glass until the mid-1970s. It appears as a molded mold on pressed glass cup plates which Pairpoint began making in the 1970s. Handpainted marks with a P inside a diamond also date from this time.

For a complete history of the various ways the authentic Pairpoint P in diamond mark was used, please see the Pairpoint entry in the Art Glass chapter.

PG in keystone

PG in a keystone is the mark of Plum Glass Co. It markets glass novelties and reissues. The Plum mark often appears with other marks including Rosso and Westmoreland from old molds put back in production.

PLATONITE

Platonite was a tradename for a line of opaque white glass made by Hazel Atlas. The word Plantonite is molded on some pieces of this line.

R–in keystone

The single letter R in a keystone is the mark of Rosso Glass, a present day glass wholesale business. Rosso specializes in reissues from old molds, antique reproductions and novelties. Rosso does not make any glass itself, but jobs out work to a number of manufactures.

Rosso owns many original vintage molds, primarily Westmoreland, but from other makers as well. The Rosso mark can

Molded R in keystone mark of Rosso Glass, a present-day glass wholesaler specializing in reissues and reproductions.

114

appear by itself or in association with other marks such as Westmoreland, which appear in the vintage molds. Many of the Rosso marks are very faint and difficult to detect. Some of the variation, of course, is due to the nature of glass manufacturing which can blur or smudge marks.

A virtually identical R in keystone mark was also registered by Rump Glass, ca. 1892. As a general rule, however, the vast majority in the market today with the R and keystone is Rosso, not from the earlier Rump.

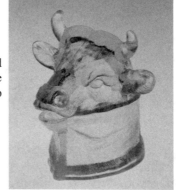

New vaseline glass bull's head mustard jar. Marked with the Rosso R in keystone mark up under the head.

Rosso distributes a wide range of new glass including a large line of new jadite glass. These shakers with color decals have the Rosso mark very faintly molded on the bottoms.

R–in shield

The shield with the letter R and four stars has been found on reproductions of Beaded Grape Medallion and Dakota patterns. Maker unknown.

Pressed Glass

RH– in shamrock or clover leaf

The molded letters RH inside either a shamrock or clover leaf is the mark of designer Robert Henry. This mark appeared in pressed glass novelties and limited edition figures produced during the 1980s.

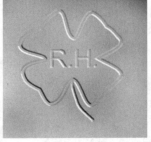 

Two marks dating from the 1980s included the letters RH. These letters appear in a shamrock, left, and a clover leaf, right.

SI

The molded letters SI represent Smithsonian Institution. These marks appear on reproductions of antique glass sold in the museum's gift shop and catalog.

S–Smith

The molded letter S, and the letter S with various other letters and symbols, make up the molded trademarks used by the L.E. Smith Glass Co.

Smith was founded in 1907 and produced a general line of pressed glass. Since the 1940s, Smith has specialized in reproductions of antique shapes and patterns. Some of Smith's current production comes from pre-1940 molds originally owned by Smith, other old molds Smith has purchased and new molds designed to produce old appearing pieces Smith has had made.

Currently, Smith is one of the major producers of glass sold in Martha Stewart's mail order catalog. Most of those pieces are made in antique shapes like covered animal dishes and antique glass colors such as jadite and brown slag. Some, but far from all, of the new glass Smith makes for Stewart is marked with one of Smith's various logos.

Smith considerably expanded its inventory of molds in antique-style patterns and shapes by purchasing 49 molds of the former L.G.

1

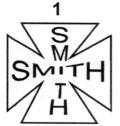

Smith arranged in a Maltese cross was used in the 1970s.

2

The letter S with a G and C is a monogram for Smith Glass Co. This dates from the 1980s. The G and S are often blurred in an actual mark, photographed, right.

3

The letter S in a circle was used as Smith mark ca. 1980-2000.

4

The cursive letter S began to be used in some Smith marks about 1997. It is replacing the other marks.

Wright glass company. The molds were purchased in 1999 when the Wright molds were liquidated at auction. Smith is gradually putting the Wright molds, like the covered melon dish shown on the next page, back in production. Pieces made from Wright molds, like other Smith glass, may or may not be marked.

The earliest Smith glass from before 1940 is not generally marked. Marks were not widely used until the 1970s and then they only appeared on certain pieces.

The first molded mark was the name Smith arranged horizontally and vertically in a Maltese-style cross (#1). The next mark, introduced in the early 1980s, is the letter S with a small G and C worked into the S forming a monogram (#2). A third mark also dates from the early 1980s through the late 1990s. This is simply the block letter S in a circle (#3). The most recent mark, a script-style upper case letter S, has been gradually replacing previous marks since about 1997 (#4).

Not all Smith products are marked. Marks on products made for outside clients, such as Stewart and others, are especially likely not to be marked.

Pressed Glass

The covered melon dish, left, is made from a mold Smith purchased at the auction of closed LG Wright glass company. Smith has made the melon dish in a brown slag glass. The Smith version is marked with a very faint script S. The new covered rabbit dish, right, is make by Smith in jadite. It is marked with a script letter S.

There is a widespread misconception that the cursive S mark on glass sold by Stewart represents Stewart. This is not correct; the cursive S is definitely the mark of L.E. Smith Glass.

Early Smith pressed glass is collectible for its own merits. Just keep in mind that Smith has a nearly 50-year habit of reissuing new glass from its old molds, both for itself as well as for private label clients such as Stewart.

St. Clair Glass Co.

The St. Clair Glass Co. was operated by John St. Clair Sr. from around 1940 to 1959. John Sr. was the head of a well known glass-making family. His descendants went on to start and operate glass businesses of their own. John marked his glass St. Clair in raised glass letters. All later St. Clair marks by John's descendants include first names and/or initials.

Joe St. Clair Art Glass

Joe St. Clair was the son of John Sr. Marks on glass by Joe St. Clair include his name arranged in a circle or on one, two or three horizontal lines. Among the best known products were Joe's reproductions of Greentown pattern toothpick holders and paperweights. All marks are in molded raised glass letters.

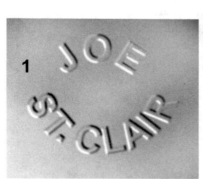
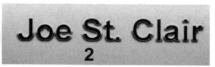

Three of the most common Joe St. Clair marks. Mark #1 found in the bottoms of paperweights. The name Joe St. Clair can appear on one, two or three lines. Examples of one and three line marks are shown in marks #2 and #3.

St. Clair–Maude and Bob

Bob is brother of Joe and son of John Sr. Maude is Bob's wife. This mark was used on pressed glass beginning ca 1974.

SM

The molded letters SM form the mark of the Sandwich Museum, Sandwich, MA. The mark appears on reproduction glass sold in the museum's gift shop and catalog.

Pressed Glass

SVPNT

A molded monogram formed by the letters SVPNT appears on a line of reproduction 19th century glass marketed by Sears Roebuck in the 1960s.

Sears marketed the glass in cooperation with Vincent Price. The line was named Vincent Price National Treasures (VPNT). An S for Sears was combined with the previous letters to produce the monogram. Glass for this series was made by Imperial Glass.

Syria–Pittsburgh 1905

This reproduction toothpick holder is marked on the front with the date "1905" and "Syria-Pittsburgh." The back has "Brown, Willcock, McComb-Niagara Falls." It is a copy of a Shrine souvenir. It is clear glass decorated in gold, ruby and white. The two-inch barrel shape has a molded wood grain in the sides. Made in various colors and decorations.

V–in a circle

Summit Art Glass has used the letter V in a circle as a mark on new glass since the 1980s. The V is for Vogelsong after the founders, Russell and Joanne Vogelsong.

Summit Art Glass owns many old molds from many prominent old factories including Fostoria, Westmoreland, Cambridge, Greentown and others. Summit also does private work for others who own molds. Summit has also made new molds of old patterns.

Letter V in circle mark of Summit Art Glass.

Few pieces are permanently marked. Many new pieces have marks that could be confused with old marks. Among these new marks are Northwood look-alikes and the McKee script mark (see Northwood and McKee in this section).

W–in a circle

The letter W in a circle– in several variations–is the mark of the L.G. Wright Glass Co. founded in the 1930s. Wright specialized in antique reproductions up until the time it closed in the mid-1990s.

Wright made no glass itself; it was only a distributor. Wright owned many molds from old glass companies and had many new molds made in copies of old patterns. Wright jobbed out production work to a variety of glass companies including Fenton, Imperial, LE Smith, and others. All of Wright's molds were sold in 1999 when the company was liquidated. Many of those molds are now back in production by other glass companies. Some new pieces now being made from the Wright molds have the Wright marks shown here. Other molds have had Wright marks removed and the new owner's mark added.

Custard tumbler by L. G. Wright with mark #1.

The similarity of Wright's W in circle marks to the Northwood N in circle mark is not coincidence. When Wright took some original Northwood molds with the N mark to Fenton to have reproductions made, Fenton refused unless the Northwood mark was altered.

First Wright mark made by altering a Northwood mark. A diagonal "leg" has been added to the original N.

W with bar below in a circle.

W in circle can also be found without the bar below the W.

Pressed Glass

LG Wright ca. 1970s-1980s custard glass plate, left, is a close copy of Northwood's original Peacock at Urn pattern. The custard plate has the Wright mark, right, that resembles an old Northwood mark with a diagonal leg added.

Wright had the marks altered by adding a diagonal leg in front of the original Northwood N (#1). Prior to this time, Wright avoided any permanent marks. In the years that followed, similar marks #2 and #3 were added. Although Wright was in business for over 60 years, only a small percentage of pieces were permanently marked.

W–in keystone, WG, Westmoreland

A letter W in a keystone (#1) was the first trademark of the Westmoreland specialty company founded in 1889 in Grapeville, PA. The W in keystone began to be used to mark glass around 1910. This mark is similar to the modern marks of Rosso Glass and Plum Glass

Keystone mark first used 1910-1930s. Don't confuse this with similar modern marks of Rosso Glass or Plum Glass.

Intertwined WG mark first used late 1940s-1982. This mark continues to appear in new products produced from original molds.

(see separate listings in this same section).

In 1924, the name of the company was abbreviated to Westmoreland Glass. A new trademark was developed combining the letters W and G into a monogram (#2). This WG mark was used on glass ca. late 1940s-1982. The company was acquired by David Grossman Designs, Inc. in 1983 which used a new mark, the letter W under the word Westmoreland (#3). The business closed in 1985.

At that time, most useable molds were sold to other glass companies, glass distributors and wholesalers. New pieces produced in the old molds can have any of the old Westmoreland marks. Some pieces, particularly the covered dishes, can have two different Westmoreland marks. It is also common for new pieces to include the name or mark of the new owner–such as Rosso Glass or Plum Glass–as well as a Westmoreland mark.

Mark first used 1982-1985. This mark continues to appear on new glass produced from original Westmoreland molds.

Weishar

Molded script mark of Weishar Enterprises. This company specializes in reissues and new shapes in old patterns. Its line of Moon and Star pattern is particularly large.

Blue Transfer Ware

Ironstone, Flow Blue, Blue Willow

Reproduction two-piece chamber pot, or slops bucket, 12-inches across handles. Flow Blue-style decoration. Marked "Victorian Ironstone" on base.

Flow Blue, Blue Willow, and Staffordshire Historical Blue are all names of various wares decorated with underglaze transfer designs in cobalt blue. Although limited reproductions of all those types have been made for many years, new blue transfer ware now occupies entire pages of reproduction wholesale catalogs. Several American wholesalers each sell over 40 new shapes; one English supplier offers nearly 100 pieces.

The majority of new marks is either directly copied from originals or based on the general appearance of originals. Perhaps the most

Marks on new transfer wares are typically very large, many two to three inches across. Original marks are rarely over one inch.

Typical authentic mark on 19th century Flow Blue ware. This mark by Ridgway.

Another typical authentic mark shown for size comparison. This mark is by Royal Doulton.

striking difference between new and old marks is size. Most new marks average two-to-three inches across regardless of the size of the piece on which they appear. Virtually no original mark approaches those dimensions. Most authentic marks on 19th century blue transfer wares are rarely over one inch in size. In other words, old marks are almost always about the size of a quarter, virtually never larger than a half-dollar. Any mark larger than a half-dollar is extremely suspicious and almost certain to be new.

The next most obvious group of new marks are those which include modern symbols such as trademark (™), registration (®) and copyright (©). The ™ and ® symbols are rarely found on pre-1950 objects. The copyright symbol is earlier, coming into widespread use ca. 1910-1915. Such symbols are particularly useful when dating the marks of potteries founded in the 19th century that continue in business today under the same name such as Masons, Ridgway, Royal Doulton, and others. Other obviously modern terms to avoid are "detergent proof," "oven safe," "dishwasher safe," and, of course, "microwave safe."

The next test is to look for generic names in the mark. No one ever

Blue Transfer Ware

walked into a 19th century china shop and said, "Excuse me, my good man, kindly direct me to the Flow Blue." Flow Blue and other descriptive names are generic terms coined by modern antique collectors. Such terms were never used in original 19th century marks. These words have been included in fake marks to suggest age and quality where none exists.

The only exception to this general rule is "Ironstone," which was originally a late-18th century trade name. By the mid-19th century, however, it entered the language as a generic term and has continued in that use to the present day. Original 19th century marks with "Ironstone" virtually never appear without a company name, such as "Mason's," "Woods & Sons," etc.

Virtually all authentic 19th century blue transfer wares–with the exception of Blue Willow–are marked with the country of origin and company name. Marks on most, but not all, authentic 19th century Flow Blue, Historical Staffordshire and Ironstone also include pattern names. Pattern and company names were an important part of original marks because they helped customers order replacements and add to a service. With few exceptions, marks on reproductions have no country of origin, no pattern name and no company name.

E. & C. Challinor Ironstone

One of the more confusing new marks on reproductions includes the name of an authentic 19th century English manufacturer, E. & C. Challinor. The new mark is virtually identical to Challinor's original 19th century

New mark is two and one-half inches wide by one and one-quarter inches tall. Old marks are rarely over one and one-half inch wide. Most, but not all, original Challinor marks include the word England. New marks found in blue underglaze. Some new marks are so dark, they appear black.

mark used ca. 1862-1891.

This mark can be particularly deceptive on new pieces that are factory-coated with a pale brown stain. The new stain duplicates the color cast frequently found on genuine 19th century ironstone.

The new Challinor marks appear on factory brown-stained pieces like this eight-inch jar with a Blue Willow transfer.

Churchill

The mark Churchill Willow was used on a line of Blue Willow china issued as a premium by a Midwest grocery chain in 1994. Similar pieces were probably available at other sources at about the same time.

The mark is applied in two forms: as a blue backstamp and impressed. The stamped mark is confusing because it includes the single word England as country of origin. Generally, England denotes manufacture between ca. 1891-1910. Most English marks after about 1910 appeared as Made in England.

Larger pieces include the words Dishwasher Safe. Smaller pieces–including many servings items–have only the marks shown here.

Marks on new Churchill Blue Willow. Printed mark in blue, left; molded mark, right. Most marks after 1910 were Made in England. This new mark is England only. No similar vintage mark known.

Blue Transfer Ware

Homestead Flo Blue

New fantasy mark in blue underglaze. No old marks include generic terms used by present day antique collectors such as "Flo Blue." Flo Blue is also spelled wrong; should be "Flow," not "Flo." No old counterpart ever existed.

New fantasy mark. Blue underglaze on reproductions.

Ironstone China–in banner

A different approach to a new mark. Vaguely similar to some 19th century marks, but no close matches known. No company name, pattern name or country of origin.

New fantasy mark, blue underglaze. "Ironstone China" in banner. Country of origin not confirmed, probably made in Asia.

Lion, crown and wreath

This mark does not have any words or numbers. It is a fantasy mark that appears only on ceramic antique reproductions from Japan. It has been in use since ca. late 1980s-early 1990s.

It appears on pieces decorated in a wide variety of styles including Flow Blue, Blue Willow, Ironstone, Imari, Delft and others. The mark has been found in dark blue, pink and brown and probably exists in other colors.

New lion, crown and wreath fantasy mark, about two and one-quarter inches across. Appears in a variety of colors on many styles of reproductions including Flow Blue, Ironstone, Imari and many others.

Ironstone China–crown

New mark, blue underglaze. Like most marks on reproductions, this mark does not include a factory name, pattern name or country of origin. "Ironstone" is a generic name and by itself is not a reliable indicator of age. This mark is somewhat similar to a pre-1850 authentic mark of Mason's Ironstone before the word Mason's was added. In the authentic early mark, Ironstone China or Patent Ironstone China in the cushion area was *impressed*. This entire look-alike new mark is printed.

New mark, blue underglaze. The word Ironstone by itself is not a reliable indicator of age.

Mason's Ironstone–modern authentic mark

Modern transfer mark of Mason's Ironstone. The Mason's name has been owned and used by GL Ashworth and Bros. since 1861. Mason's remains a trademark used through the present day.

Printed marks in use today are generally similar to 19th century printed marks. Marks after 1891 include England; marks after about

Similar to 19th century mark but now includes the © symbol. England or Made in England generally did not appear within the old mark as it does here. This authentic mark includes the company name Mason's, the pattern name Quail and country of origin, England.

Blue Transfer Ware

1910 include Made in England. Modern Mason's marks also generally include the © symbol.

Note that Made in England within this ca. 1990s mark is included in the cushion. Generally, England or Made in England, did not appear within the cushion until about mid-20th century. Pre-WW II marks usually have England or Made in England down below the mark. Authentic marks are the same color as the transfer decoration.

Mason's Ironstone– vintage authentic mark

Typical authentic mark of Mason's Ironstone used from the last quarter of 19th century virtually unchanged through the late 1930s.

England appears below the mark, not within the cushion. The use of England dates this mark between roughly 1891 and 1910. After about 1910, the country mark was generally Made in England.

Vista is the pattern name. These transfer marks appear in the same color as the transfer decoration.

The heavy earthenware called Ironstone was patented by Charles James Mason in 1813. Charles and his brother George were the original makers who began Mason's Patent Ironstone China. The company went bankrupt in 1848. Mold and patterns were sold and passed through various owners until 1861. At that time, Mason's remaining molds, patterns and trademarks were purchased by GL

Typical authentic Mason's mark, ca. 1891-1910. The same mark with Made in England was used up through the 1930s.

The mark shown at left appears on this small berry bowl. The pattern, or transfer name, is Vista, which also appears in the mark.

Ashworth & Bros. The Mason's Ironstone remained in control of that firm through the late 1960s. Today, Mason's Ironstone is now controlled by the Wedgwood Group and the Mason's name is still in use (see typical new mark on the previous page).

Mayfayre Staffordshire

Mark found on reproductions of various types of blue transfer decorated wares. This example found on doll-sized tea set in Flow Blue.

New mark, no old counterpart known. Mark has been found in two colors, gold and blue.

New doll-sized teapot with Mayfayre Staffordshire mark.

Ringtons, Ringtons Limited

Ringtons LTD was an English tea merchant. It commissioned English potters to make ceramic tea-related items such as tea caddies, teapots and other pieces with the Ringtons' name. Most of the original Ringtons ceramic pieces were decorated in the Blue Willow pattern

Old

As of early 2002, the original Ringtons mark, left, that appears on authentic teapots has not been reproduced. Note that "Maling Ware" is included at the bottom. Maling Ware does not appear in any new Ringtons mark.

Blue Transfer Ware

and are highly sought collectibles.

Reproductions have been made since at least the 1980s and maybe earlier. New pieces are made in shapes identical to originals and new marks are very close to original marks.

This was the first new mark put on Ringtons reproductions. It did not include Newcastle upon Tyne; original marks did. New eight-inch Blue Willow tea jar, right, is identical to an original shape.

Latest Ringtons reproduction mark since about 2000, now includes Newcastle upon Tyne just like originals. This new mark is now identical to an original Ringtons mark used 1928 to 1955. Inside of new lid is not glazed. Old lid is glazed and is marked with RT monogram. Mark appears on the new eight-inch Blue Willow tea jar, right, identical in shape to an original Ringtons jar.

Blue Transfer Ware

Underside of lid from new Rington Tea jar. Inside of new lids is not glazed; missing RT monogram discussed, right.

Original RT monogram is printed underglaze on the inside of almost all authentic lids on old Ringtons jars and teapots. Old lids are glazed on the inside. Most new lids like the one, left, are unglazed bisque.

Staffordshire Ironstone

New mark in black transfer found on a reproduction pitcher and bowl. No exact old counterpart known, but similar to many vintage marks using a crown.

Stanley Touraine

New Touraine pattern Flow Blue marked Stanley Pottery Co. has a mark almost identical to the vintage original mark. The new mark is missing one important feature and that is the word "England." Both new and old marks contain the same British Registry number.

New Stanley Pottery Co. mark without the word England.

Stanley Pottery mark on original Touraine includes the word England.

Blue Transfer Ware

Swan–and banner

This new swan mark has been found on a number of reproductions with Flow Blue-style decorations including the pitcher shown below. The new mark is based on a genuine old mark of T. Rathbone, Newfield Pottery, Tunstall, England, ca. 1898-1923. The old mark, shown below right, dates from about 1912.

New swan mark in blue transfer. This mark appears on Flow Blue-style reproductions including the pitcher shown on the next page.

Genuine old mark of T. Rathbone, Newfield Pottery, Tunstall, England, ca. 1898-1923. Rathbone made a number of patterns in Flow Blue.

This new Flow Blue pitcher has the new swan mark discussed and shown above. Pattern is a close, but not exact, match for an original pattern named Trentham made by T. Rathbone, Newfield Pottery.

Victoria Ironstone–China

This new mark is based on a loose copy of the British Royal Arms. It is applied to reproductions of Flow Blue, Ironstone and other imitations of English Victorian-era pottery. The mark appears in dark blue underglaze. Usually very large, generally two or more inches.

Victoria Ironstone–England

Not all reproductions come from Asia. This "Victoria Ironstone" mark is used by Blakeney Pottery LTD, England, on reproductions. It is a modified copy of the British Royal Arms. This mark has been in use since 1968. Note that this mark includes the word England.

Victoria Stone Ware Ironstone

A variation of the many new marks that include the word "Victoria." There is no known old counterpart.

Stone Ware in center shield, Victoria in banner. Very large, over two inches tall. Underglaze in blue. No company name or country of origin. Made in China.

Victoria Ware Ironstone

Another new mark based on the British Royal Arms. This mark appears on reproductions from China. One of the most widely appearing marks on new blue transfer wares. Found on a broad range of shapes including pitchers and wash basins, chamber sets and other large pieces, as well as small accessories.

Legibility varies considerably. Some marks so smudged as to appear almost as a solid block of dark blue.

Latin motto in center shield; Victoria Ware in lower banner; Ironstone below. No country or company name. This mark has been found up to three inches wide. Thick glaze blurs mark underneath.

Royal Dux

Two Royal Dux 12" horses. Both have the same impressed shape number, yet one is about twice as old as the other. In this chapter we look at the marks found on Royal Dux products.

Duxer Porzellanmanufaktur, or Dux Porcelain Manufactory, was started in 1860 by Eduard Eichler in what was then Duchov, Bohemia. The high quality pottery and porcelain figures produced there are now generally referred to by the abbreviated name, "Royal Dux."

The problem facing collectors is that many original 19th century molds have remained in production throughout the company's 150 year history. With vintage 19th century Royal Dux selling for up to several thousand dollars, modern pieces are often offered, either deliberately or through ignorance, as much older than they really are.

Royal Dux products can be divided into four broad periods of production generally separated by wars and political upheaval: 1860 to WW I; 1919 to WW II; 1947 to 1990 and from 1990 to the present. From 1860 to WW II, ca. 1939, the company operated under the original name Duxer Porzellanmanufaktur, commonly called Royal Dux. After WW II, around 1946-47, the factory was nationalized by the Soviet Union and renamed Duchovsky Porcelain. The company returned to private ownership with the collapse of the Soviet Union in

First period, ca. 1860-WW I

Line drawing of the oldest raised triangle mark. Royal Dux Bohemia appears around an oval with the letter E. The letter impressed in the triangle changes over the years.

Photo of the earliest raised pink triangle mark. Note that all lettering is impressed. Triangles are made of pink clay.

ROYAL DUX

These are three other marks which may appear with the early raised pink E triangle or may appear alone. These marks are usually impressed.

1990. Since 1990, molds and variations of company marks from earlier periods have continued to be used as Royal Dux continues production into the 21st century.

Royal Dux introduced one of the most distinctive marks ever placed on porcelain, a raised triangle of pink clay. All factory-applied pink triangles–whether from the 19th, 20th or 21st century–are made from a separate piece of pink clay. The pink clay is applied to the base of Royal Dux white clay bodies. The two separate pieces are fused together during firing. There is virtually never the slightest seam or gap between the pink clay of the triangle and the white clay of the piece to which the triangle is applied.

Before WW I, pink triangles were generally, but not always, left in a bisque, or unglazed, finish. Most Art Nouveau figures in matte glaze, for example, usually have bisque triangles. After WW I, Art Deco figures entirely glazed in a high gloss occasionally have glazed triangles. Pieces with gloss glazes after 1950, especially after 1980, are more likely to have some glaze on the triangle. Although bisque triangles are the general rule, there is considerable variation over the years.

Second period, ca. 1919-WW II

After WW I, Bohemia, home of the Dux factory, was united with Moravia and Slovakia to form the country of Czechoslovakia. Around 1919, "Made in Czechoslovakia" began to be added to Royal Dux marks. Made in Czechoslovakia may appear separately or joined to the pre-1918 marks. The letter E remained in the pink triangle, along with Royal Dux Bohemia around the oval.

Pre-1918 marks with Made In Czechoslovakia added.
Exact appearance and location of marks will vary.

Factory triangles are all roughly the same size, about one-half inch per side and raised about one-sixteenth inch thick, and rarely more than one-eighth inch thick. Size varies slightly because some original triangles were slightly deformed when damp.

Appearing in all genuine factory-applied raised pink triangles, regardless of age, is "Royal Dux Bohemia." That lettering appears around an oval shape in the center of the triangle. A crosshatch, or grid-like pattern, is at the top of the oval. Even though the country of Bohemia disappeared at the end of WW I, Royal Dux Bohemia remains in the mark to this day.

All factory-applied pink triangles, new or old, are generally very high quality. You almost never find a blurred, indistinct or illegible impression in factory-applied triangles. Virtually all factory-applied triangles have sharp, clear lettering impressed to an equal depth.

Each of the four periods of production can be roughly identified by changes in marks. In the first period, 1860 to WW I, the letter E is

Third period, ca.late 1947-1990

The pottery was nationalized by the Soviet Union at the end of WW II. The letter E is removed from the pink triangle and replaced by the letter D. Royal Dux Bohemia continues to appear around the oval. The triangle remains the same color and size.

Some pieces made in the early 1950s have an M rather than a D in the pink triangles. Very few of the M pieces have ever appear in Western markets.

Stamped in black, blue or dark green ink. Triangle with D, Royal Dux Bohemia. "Hand Painted, Made in Czechoslovakia" around triangle. After WW II.

impressed in the center of the pink triangle. E represents Eichler, the founder's surname. The letter in the center of triangles changes over the years. It's important to keep in mind that E is the earliest. A convenient way to remember this is by word association: E is for early. The great majority of authentic factory-applied triangles from the first production period are unglazed.

Following the end of WW I, Bohemia, the home of Royal Dux, was united with Slovakia and Moravia to form a new nation, Czechoslovakia. This change was reflected in the phrase "Made in Czechoslovakia" which being appearing in Royal Dux marks around 1919. The letter E continued to be impressed in the center of the pink triangle and "Royal Dux Bohemia" impressed around the oval.

Made in Czechoslovakia can appear joined to other Royal Dux marks or can appear separately at a distance from other marks.

Fourth period, since 1990

Typical marks used since 1990. Line drawing, left; photo, right. Note the introduction of Czech Republic rather than Czechoslovakia. The registered symbol and Hand Painted Made in Czech Republic are black, remainder of mark is blue. The number 1853 below the triangle should not be confused with a date.

Marks used since the early 1990s have been very confusing. The letter D once again returns to the center of the pink triangle replacing the M. The modern symbols for copyright, ©, and registration, ®, also begin to be used. The new national name Czech Republic appears in many, but far from all, new marks. Many new pieces since the late 1990s have also been marked Made in Czechoslovakia, exactly the same wording as used ca. 1919-1939. A gold foil label has also been used since the early 1990s.

Typical colors for stamped ink marks include green and a reddish-pink.

At the end of WW II, Russia, then the Soviet Union, continued to occupy east-European countries its troops held when Germany surrendered. This included Czechoslovakia. Russia nationalized almost all Czechoslovakian industries including Royal Dux. Around 1946-47, the factory was renamed Duchcovsky Porcelain after the regional name of Duchov.

The letter E was removed from the center of the pink triangle at this time and replaced by the letter D. Royal Dux Bohemia continues to appear around the oval. The triangle is still a separate piece of pink

New six and one-half inch vase made between 2000-2001; white bodied porcelain with transfer floral decoration and gold trim. Green backstamp Royal Dux Made in Czechoslovakia, upper left. Also gold foil label, Royal Dux Bohemia.

Three-inch frog paperweight, white with high-gloss glaze and trimmed in gold. Retail price in 1995 was $24. Marked with a black backstamp, middle, Made in Czech Republic, ® and triangle. Also with raised pink triangle, right.

clay applied to a white clay body. Made in Czechoslovakia again appears in marks sometime in the early 1950s.

Some products made in the early 1950s have an M rather than a D in the pink triangle. Very few of these pieces have been seen in Western markets. For all practical purposes, the letter D is the dominant letter in the vast majority of pink triangles since WW II.

The collapse of the Soviet Union in the early 1990s ushered in tremendous changes in eastern Europe. Royal Dux returned to private ownership and Czechoslovakia changed its name to Czech Republic. With all these changes, production since 1990 is by far the most difficult to accurately date by marks alone.

The most significant change was in the general policy regarding marks. Rather than going forward with totally new marks, the factory brought back marks used in the past. The letter inside the triangle–in both printed marks and the raised pink mark–continued to be the letter

Royal Dux

Running deer, about 12-inches long; high gloss glaze, ca. 1990s. Marked on base with raised pink D-triangle and Made in Czechoslovakia in black backstamp.

D. Printed marks begin to include not only "Made in Czech Republic" but also "Made in Czechoslovakia" previously used only on pre-WW II pieces. Pieces made since the mid-1990s in original molds and carrying the old-appearing marks can be difficult to separate from 19th and early 20th century originals.

Here are a few general guidelines that will help you identify most 1990s pieces. First, any piece marked with the modern copyright symbol, ©, or modern registered symbol, ®, are from the 1990s. Any piece marked Czech Republic cannot be older than 1990-1991 at most. Pieces with a gold foil label with a letter D in the center are also from the 1990s. Pieces marked Made in Czechoslovakia–made before or after 1990–can in no instance possibly date before 1919 at the earliest. Czechoslovakia was created at the end of WW I, ca. 1918-1919. Any piece with a D impressed in the pink triangle cannot date any earlier than the late 1940s.

However, neither "Made in Czechoslovakia" or a D impressed in the pink triangle are guarantees of age. Both of those markings have been used in the 1990s and continue to be in use as of 2001. The new two-handled vase on the previous page, for example, is marked Made in Czechoslovakia, but was made in 2002. There is also a raised pink triangle with the impressed letter D on the frog on the same page .

Generally, pieces with a letter E impressed in a raised pink triangle with no marks other than shape numbers or decorators' marks, are still very likely to have been made before 1919. Pink triangles on these pieces are generally bisque. Pieces with E impressed in a raised pink triangle and also marked "Made in Czechoslovakia" impressed, not

New sixteen-inch vase with Art Nouveau nude. Marked with forged triangle above which has the letter E in the center. This triangle is painted pink; all original triangles are made of pink clay. Note how the color in the triangle fades on the left side.

Forged raised pink triangle above is a thick, rough-textured slab found on the figure at left. Original pink triangles are rarely over one-eighth inch thick. This new triangle has the letter E in the center.

backstamped, most likely date between the world wars, 1919-1939.

Another, but less objective, test is the quality of the finish. Most matte glazed pieces from before WW II, especially before 1900, are velvety smooth. Surfaces of pieces made after WW II tend to be rougher. This test only works on matte finished pieces, though, and you need to be familiar with originals. This test does not apply to pieces with gloss glazes.

Pieces with a D impressed in a raised pink triangle with "Made

Royal Dux

in Czechoslovakia" applied as either a transfer or ink stamp, need to be examined very, very carefully. Although "Made in Czechoslovakia" was first used ca. 1919-1939, that same mark is again being applied with decals and stamps on new pieces made since 1990s.

Besides separating confusing marks and pieces made at the Royal Dux factory, buyers must also contend with fakes and forgeries. Some fakes are quite ambitious, going so far as to copy the raised pink triangles like the examples shown in this chapter. Both forgeries have Made in Bohemia and the letter E impressed into raised pink triangles, similar to the genuine Royal Dux triangles used 1860-1918.

There are several clues to help you detect these and most other forged triangles. First, look at the color. All original raised pink triangles are made of pink clay; the pink color is throughout the body of the triangle. No authentic factory-made pink triangles old or new are painted. Letters in genuine triangles are impressed to almost exactly the same depth. The depth to which letters are impressed on most new triangles can vary greatly.

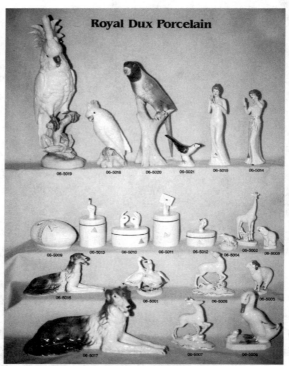

Catalog page of Royal Dux products from mid-1990s.
Many of these pieces have a raised pink triangle.

A forged "Loetz" mark made with a diamond-tip pen. All original engraved Loetz marks were rotary engraved; none were made with a diamond-tip pen.

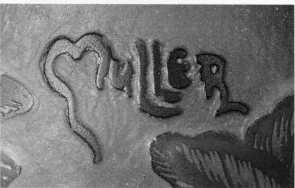

New "Muller" raised glass signature on new cameo glass from China. This is identical to an original Muller mark.

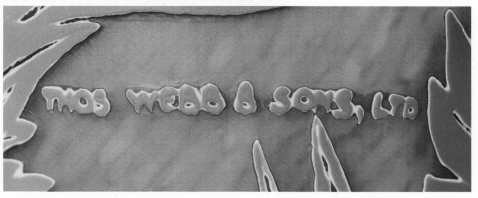

New raised glass signature on new cameo glass from China, "THOS WEBB & SONS, LTD." No authentic Webb cameo was marked in this manner. See the Cameo chapter for authentic Webb marks.

An authentic Tiffany engraved mark and original LCT monogram paper label on ground pontil. All authentic Tiffany glass has a ground pontil.

A fake Tiffany black and white paper label with "LCT" monogram applied to rough, or scarred, pontil.

Another fake Tiffany black and white paper label with "Tiffany Glass and Decorating Co." monogram. This is a very poor quality photocopy. The outside edge of the label is irregular and shows signs of being hand cut. Original labels were die-cut in perfect circles.

A molded "WG" mark of Westmoreland Glass first used in the late 1940s. This mark continues to appear in new products produced from original molds. This mark is in the bottom of a covered animal dish made in 2000.

The mark of "E & C Challinor," an authentic 19th century English pottery, as it now appears on reproductions. Note the background is tinted brown to suggest age.

Many fake marks on blue transfer wares, such as flow blue, are very large, and can range from two to three inches across.

Marks on original blue transfer wares, such as this authentic Royal Doulton backstamp, are rarely over one inch across.

A faked "Royal Dux" raised triangle mark. Original triangles are pink clay with the color running throughout the triangle. This forgery is white clay painted pink. Some paint has worn away, revealing the white clay.

A fake "Limoges" mark on ceramic reproductions. This mark is found in several colors. No old counterpart.

This reproduction hatpin holder is marked on the base with the "Limoges China" mark shown in the photo above.

This forged "RS Prussia" mark was hand painted on an old, but originally unmarked, vase. All original RS Prussia marks were applied as transfers, not hand painted.

This is a new "Buffalo Pottery" mark found on current reproductions. This is an Asian water buffalo, not an American bison which appears in genuine Buffalo Pottery marks. Note the use of the date 1911 at the bottom of the mark.

The new Buffalo Pottery mark shown in the photo above appears on this new 10-inch ceramic plate advertising J. Pauleys Cigars.

149

A reproduction Etruscan Majolica water pitcher in sunflower pattern. This new pitcher has a blurred Etruscan mark as shown in the photo below.

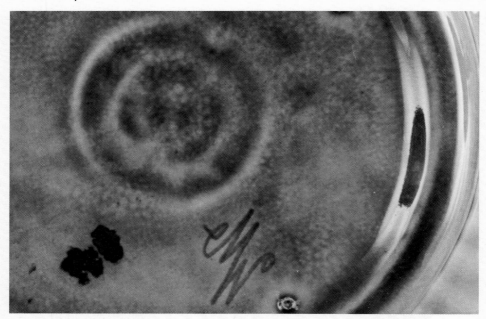

The Etruscan Majolica mark as found on the sunflower pitcher. Also note the incised "MW" at the bottom, which is the mark of Majolica Works which makes the new pitcher. All pieces with this "MW" are new.

This reproduction cup and saucer is decorated in the mid-19th century style marked "KPM."

This is the facsimile "KPM" mark on the new cup and saucer in the photo shown above. These marks are applied at the factory. They arrive at the wholesaler with a removable "Made in China" paper label.

Reproduction "RC Nippon" mark found on new ceramics. The entire mark is one color, a dull green.

The original RC Nippon mark is always two colors. The words "Hand Painted" are red; "RC Nippon" is green.

This authentic oval mark of Red Wing Union Stoneware Co., Red Wing, Minn., is found on vintage stoneware made from 1906 through the 1930s.

This is the new mark of Red Wing Stoneware Co. of Red Wing, Minn., made since the mid-1980s. The company today makes copies of a wide range of vintage Red Wing stoneware. Most new pieces have this mark.

This forged "Rv" mark is on the new La Rose vase shown in the photo below. It is very thin and rubber stamped in pale blue ink. Original marks are much bolder and appear in a dark blue or black ink.

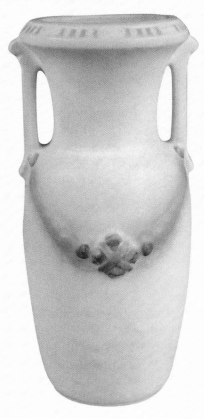

This is a reproduction Roseville Pottery 9-inch vase in the La Rose pattern. This piece is marked with a faked "Rv" mark shown in the photo above.

A new 4-inch pottery tile very similar to a Grueby Pottery vintage original. It is mounted in a new quarter-sawn oak frame similar to frames used during the Arts and Crafts era.

The new Grueby-like tile in the photo above marked "Ephraim Pottery USA" on the back. If the back of the tile is covered, you won't be able to see this new mark.

A new Little Red Riding Hood cookie jar. These new jars are now marked exactly like the Hull Pottery originals. You need to measure the height to separate old from new.

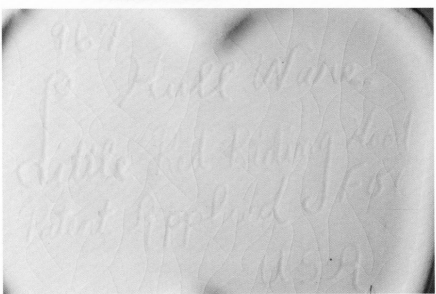

This impressed "Hull" mark on the bottom of reproduction Little Red Riding Hood cookie jars is virtually identical to the original mark.

A reproduction Baby Elephant with Ice Cream Cone cookie jar. This new jar is marked "W-8 Brush McCoy" on the base. The original is marked "Brush Pottery," not Brush McCoy.

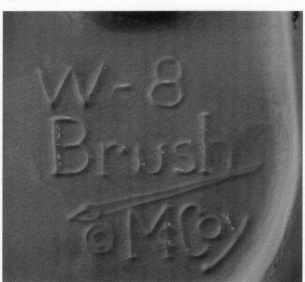

This is the mark on the base of the Elephant cookie jar in the photo above. "Brush McCoy" marks appear only on reproductions, not on vintage cookie jars.

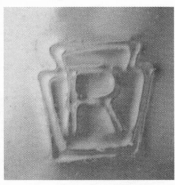

Molded "R" in keystone mark of Rosso Glass. This mark appears in a new piece of vaseline glass. Rosso Glass sells a wide range of new glass made in old colors from new and old molds.

This letter "G" in diamond mark with "925" and "STERLING" appears only on new silver reproductions, primarily match safes. There is no old counterpart to this mark.

A new sterling silver match safe with the new letter "G in diamond 925 STERLING" mark. This new piece is a close copy of a vintage original made for the Benevolent and Protective Order of the Elks (BPOE).

Before strict trade laws, many manufacturers marked non-sterling goods with confusing names that suggested sterling quality. These marks all appear on vintage originals made ca. 1885-1915, but only on non-silver alloys. These include Bristol Silver, in the photo above; Nearsilver, photo at bottom left; and Sterline, photo at bottom right.

A reproduction figural watch fob shaped like an early baseball catcher's mitt.

The new catcher's mitt in the photo above is marked "Winchester Sporting Goods The Winchester Store." Winchester is a highly collectible name and has inspired many reproductions.

A fake "Keen Kutter" paper label applied to a kitchen scale. The seller claimed the label was original, applied at the time of manufacture. If that is true, how did the paint underneath the label get chipped? It's obvious the new label has been recently applied over an already chipped background.

A reproduction 8-inch figural bulldog humidor marked "Xomex."

This impressed mark "XOMEX" appears on the reproduction humidor in the photo above. This example was found with a removable "Made in China" paper label.

China and Porcelain

Many of the confusing marks on reproductions of china and porcelain are *importer's* marks. That is to say, the marks were designed or requested by the importing *customer* rather than required by laws regulating international trade. Legal requirements are fully met by removable paper labels bearing the true country of origin. It is perfectly legal, for example, for a piece to be permanently marked Royal Vienna or Prussia, as long as the piece has a Made in China paper label.

This is one reason that many of these marks cannot be found in books with antique marks–no old counterparts ever existed. True, some new marks include *place names* and *symbols* found in genuine old marks–such as Prussia, Vienna, and "beehives,"–but those features are included to suggest age and quality, rather than to accurately identify their true source.

Marks may also include words such as "Handpainted" when the decoration is actually applied by transfer, not painted. Other words such as "Genuine," "Authentic" and "Original," are almost always the sign of a reproduction or reissue.

Besides new backstamps, many reproductions also have misleading information within the decorations. These include facsimile artist "signatures" and spurious dates.

Always beware of generic names such as Delfts, Staffordshire, Flo Blue and others. These are words used by modern collectors to describe *categories* of wares, not specific companies. Reproduction manufacturers often include those words in marks to capitalize on their name recognition among collectors of antiques.

China and Porcelain

Anchor

There are a great many new and fake marks that use an anchor without any accompanying words, symbols or country. As a general rule, most old vintage anchors are either impressed or hand painted. New anchors are generally stamped or a decal. Be particularly careful with gold anchor marks applied over the glaze. Many new pieces have these anchors in imitation of old Chelsea marks.

A & C Bavaria

This new mark appears on reproductions made in Japan for American reproduction wholesalers. This example is in gold, but is probably in other colors as well. The mark found on many different shapes including the covered jar shown here. Pieces with the A & C Bavaria mark also frequently include the facsimile signature A. Koch. The Koch signature is virtually identical to a late 19th century A. Koch signature found on vintage grape pattern transfers.

New A & C, Bavaria mark, above, is a close copy of a ca. 1902 original mark shown below. The new mark appears in gold on the covered grape-decorated jar, upper right. Grape design includes facsimile A. Koch signature, right.

Old

Old mark, J & C, Bavaria, Jaeger & Co, Bavaria, ca. 1902. This old mark appears on virtually identical shapes of china with similar decorations including a grape pattern very close to the one on the new box shown above.

162

Arnart

Arnart Imports is a New York import firm, ca. 1957 to present. It handled many antique reproductions, ca. 1960s-1990s. The company used several marks.

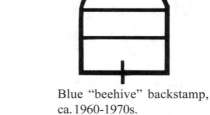

Blue "beehive" backstamp, ca. 1960-1970s.

Arrows backstamp is made of wavy lines to imitate hand painting, ca. 1960-1970s.

Registered company logo, 1990.

Bone dish with blue beehive backstamp, classical style transfer decoration.

ARNART 5th Ave
Backstamp under glaze, ca. 1960-1970s.

Aynsley

Mark of John Aynsley & Sons, London, England, ca. 1960s-1970s. Now a division of Waterford.

Beehive marks

Marks commonly called "beehive" are actually shields–they have been turned upside down by mistaken collectors. Because most of the original shield marks are associated with age and quality, modern manufacturers capitalize on this belief by including such marks on their reproductions.

The vast majority of original 19th century shield marks were

China and Porcelain

The words Royal Vienna orient the "beehive" with the dome toward the top. This mark is *stamped* in blue.

An authentic *handpainted* shield, oriented in the correct position by the handpainted characters below.

handpainted on some of the very finest porcelain. Imitations of those original marks are almost always found as transfers or backstamps.

Belleek

Fine porcelain has been produced under the Belleek name since 1857 when pottery began in the County Fermanagh, Ireland. The basic mark is an Irish harp, an Irish wolfhound and a castle tower. BELLEEK appears below in an arch; at both ends of the arch are sprigs of shamrocks.

Periodic variations to this basic mark—including color changes, additions and deletions of words and symbols—help collectors establish dates of production.

With the exception of Belleek parian from the mid-19th century which was either impressed "BELLEEK" or "BELLEEK, CO FERMANAGH" or with the first hound/harp/tower mark, all Belleek porcelain is marked with the stamps shown below.

First Black Mark, 1863-1890
Belleek appears in arch. Printed primarily in black, but also limited use in other color. This mark also impressed in parian wares.

Second Black Mark, 1891-1926
A banner with Co. Fermanagh Ireland is added. Printed in black.

Third Black Mark, 1926-1946
A disc with Deanta In Eirinn
(made in Ireland) and the British
Registry number 0857 was
added. Printed in black.

First Green Mark, 1946-1955
The same as the Third black
mark, but printed in green.

Second Green Mark, 1955-1965
The R in circle American registry
mark is added. Printed in green.

Third Green Mark, 1965-1979
Co Fermanagh is removed from
the banner, Ireland remains.
Printed in green.

Since 1980
The disc Deanta in Eirinn is
removed from the mark.
Printed in gold. Commonly
referred to as First Gold Mark.

Bareuther Bavaria

Exact source unknown. Found on reproduction game and portrait plates sold by USA reproduction wholesalers from the 1960s through the early 1980s. This mark is yellow lettering on black.

China and Porcelain

Baronet

This mark was used by an American importer, Fischer, Bruce and Co. It appears on many types of ceramic products made in antique styles since the 1950s including a series of portrait plates.

Booths

Booths Pottery, Tunstall, England. Now part of Royal Doulton. This mark is printed on pottery.

Boucher

Close up of a modern transfer with "Boucher" signature with the date 1759. Note the pattern of dots produced by modern color printing used to make the transfer. This signature with various dates is found on many reproductions.

Brandenburg

A backstamp used on antique reproductions made in Japan ca. 1960-1980. Brandenburg suggests a German origin, but no known old counterpart. Anchors were used in many vintage marks.

Burleigh Ironstone

Burgess & Leigh, Burslem, England. This mark is used on heavy dinnerware in antique-like shapes, ca. 1970s.

Buffalo Pottery

Fake Buffalo Pottery marks have been found on new 10-inch porcelain plates. One new mark is simply the word "Buffalo," the other new mark is more elaborate and includes a "buffalo." The second mark is similar in form to an original mark used by Buffalo Pottery Co. of Buffalo, New York.

Original Buffalo Pottery marks were almost always underglaze printed transfers. The animal on new marks is an Asian water buffalo. Authentic Buffalo Pottery marks use an American bison.

The original Buffalo Pottery was one of the few American potters to consistently place permanent date marks on virtually all products. This policy was begun at the start of production in 1903 and continued until handwork was entirely replaced by mechanization during the 1940s. Dates on virtually all original pre-1940 production were applied as part of the larger printed transfer company mark. The new dates are handpainted.

Note that the new mark with the buffalo is "dated" with 1911 below the mark. An original Buffalo Pottery mark of the same year is shown for comparison.

New   **Old**

The animal on new marks is an Asian water buffalo, left. Authentic Buffalo Pottery marks use an American bison, right. The new mark is dated 1911. Original marks are applied in transfers; the fakes are handpainted.

BUFFALO

Another new handpainted mark, the single word BUFFALO.

Reproduction 10-inch plate with fake Buffalo Pottery buffalo mark. Plate advertises J. Pauleys Hambone Cigars.

China and Porcelain

Chintz

English chintz has been reproduced since the mid-1990s by the same factories which made the vintage 1920-1950s pieces. At least two of these firms, James Kent, which made Old Foley, and Grimwades, maker of Royal Winton, use backstamps on new pieces that could be confused with marks appearing on vintage pieces.

Shown here are some typical examples from those makers. New pieces are being brought out all the time and you need to pay close attention to which marks are being used on the reproductions and reissues. Many backstamps on vintage pieces were stamped with ink and often smudged. Many new marks are applied as decals and appear perfectly regular and uniform.

(For more on chintz, visit www.chintznet.com/susan and order the *Charlton Standard Catalogue of Chintz* by Susan Scott. Foley and Winton backstamps appear coutesy of Susan Scott.)

James Kent Old Foley backstamps

Mark found on 1999 pieces of Old Foley by James Kent. James Kent may also appear in middle with Old Foley in the banner below.

Backstamp with monograms date from 1999 or later when factories began to identify their decorators with special marks.

Backstamp used by James Kent in the late 1980s.

1950s James Kent backstamp.

New

James Kent mark, left, appears on the reproduction chintz scuttle shaving mug, right. Note the line "18th century Chintz" in the new mark.

Grimwades Royal Winton backstamps

Old

Original Royal Winton by Grimwades Art Deco-style mark stamped in black ink, slightly under one-inch across. Similar reproduction marks are three-quarter inch and one and one-quarter inch.

Old

If the Art Deco-style back-stamp has a large A (arrow), you can be reasonably sure the piece is vintage. The "A" was first used about 1943 and remained part of some backstamps until the 1960s.

New

New Art Deco-styled backstamp on some items produced late 1997 through early 1998. Letters "LTD." have been added under Grimwades. In February 1998 the factory added "1995" to the backstamp to prevent confusion. See mark at right.

New

New Art Deco-style back-stamp with "1995" added in February 1998.

169

China and Porcelain

New

Blue backstamp used on new Julia produced for Clementine Rusk of California. It is suspected that some of these marks may have been altered in the secondary market to resemble vintage marks.

Cowboy China–Western themes

One of the most popular of original western-theme dinnerwares is a multicolored pattern called Rodeo. Originals were made by Wallace China Company of Los Angeles, California, for the M.C. Wentz Company of Pasadena, California. Wentz marketed the china in its full line of western-theme housewares under the name Westward Ho. Originals are marked both Westward Ho and Wallace China. New pieces do not include Wallace China.

A facsimile signature of the pattern's designer, Till Goodan,

Original Westward Ho Rodeo dinner plate by Wallace China, 1943-1964. Originals are marked with the Westward Ho logo, Made in California and Wallace China. The original designer's name, Till Goodan, appears on *most but not all* of the old pieces. Be aware that an unidentified maker in the early 1990s made some *new* pieces with the Goodan signature. The original backstamp is the most reliable way to authentic originals.

170

New Westward Ho Rodeo dinnerware brought out in the early 1990s, left. Marked with the new backstamp, right. New mark does not include Wallace China. Compare to original mark previous page.

New Little Buckaroo china, left, also copied from 1940-1950s originals. Backstamp, right, does not include Wallace China.

appears on most, but not all, of the old pieces. But don't use this as a test of age–Goodan signatures also appear on some of the new.

There are also new look-alike patterns, new patterns created to generally resemble the style and look of old vintage patterns. A *new* western pattern called Skyranch, for example, is very similar to old El Rancho made in the 1940s-1950s by Wallace China. Original pieces are decorated with line drawings of typical western images–brands, spurs, cattle, etc.–in a deep maroon on a tan background.

New skyranch can be identified by the crossed branding irons backstamp with the R and S.

The best way to tell many of the new western and cowboy pieces from the old is by the backstamp. Most old patterns generally carry

 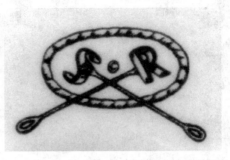

Look-alike new western pattern Skyranch, left, is similar to a pattern named El Rancho made by Wallace China in ca. 1940-1950s. New Skyranch has branching iron mark, SR, right. Original El Rancho has the old Wallace backstamp.

marks of companies no longer in business such as Wallace China. Keep in mind that some new backstamps, like Westward Ho, are similar to original marks but not exact copies. In those cases, you need to match original factory marks very carefully.

New Westward Ho Rodeo pattern dinnerware was made by True West Pottery. Its logo may appear on some pieces.

Backstamp of Cow Camp China on new china with cowboy and western-related designs. Pipestone is a pattern name. Most of its patterns are from new designs, not copies of vintage patterns

Original Wallace China back-stamp used up through 1964.

Currier & Ives

A series of ceramics sold by an American reproduction wholesaler are marked "Currier and Ives" in the decoration. The title of the plate precedes the mark. Backstamps on these plates are usually custom names requested by the importer.

Most of the Currier and Ives-marked pieces were plates

Script "Hunting for deer, Currier & Ives" on front of reproduction plates. The script is a transfer, not handpainted. No old counterpart to this mark.

sold from the 1970s through the late 1980s. The original 19th century lithography firm of Currier and Ives never issued any similar ceramic pieces.

DECOR/VIEK

"From the kiln of DECOR/ VIEK" is a mark found on reproduction shaving mugs. This example includes the original price tag from Abercrombie and Fitch. The title of the shaving mug is Cable Car visible in the tag.

Delft, Delfts

Generic Delft plaques and plates have been offered in antique reproduction wholesale catalogs virtually unchanged for more than 30 years. The great majority of the reproduction Delft-style pieces in the market do not have any old counterpart. They are entirely fantasy pieces invented for interior decorators and antique reproduction wholesalers. Current wholesale price for new 16-inch plaques is $16 to $20.

Over the years, reproduction Delft

New

China and Porcelain

New

This new 16-inch diameter platter and the one on the previous page are from antique reproduction wholesalers. Similar pieces have been sold for over 40 years. No old counterparts to pieces exist. They were designed solely for the decorating and reproduction trade.

has carried a number of backstamps and marks that suggest the pieces are much older than their recent manufacture. Most of these new marks, however, are also fantasy marks with no old authentic counterparts.

Separating new from old is fairly simple. First, as a general rule, any mark that includes the word "Delfts" with an "s" is new—that is, less than 30 to 40 years old. Any piece marked "Delft," was probably made in the 20th century or late 19th century at the very earliest.

New

Old

MADE IN HOLLAND

Royal Sphinx Maastricht was a new mark, ca. mid-1970 to late 1980s. Mark includes Royal Sphinx Maastricht, Made in Holland, Delfts. Signature under Sphinx is P. Regout. Note use of word "Delfts" with letter "s." This particular variation is loosely based on the genuinely old Royal Sphinx mark, right.

Authentic mark of De Sphinx pottery of Maastricht, Holland, ca. 1890-1920s . Founded by Petrus Regout (P. Regout) 1836. Appears on a variety of ceramic wares.

New

New

Royal Copenhagen, Boch was a new mark ca. 1960s-1980s. Made for Royal Copenhagen by Boch is stamped in dark blue ink. Note use of word "Delfts" with the letter "s."

New mark, used since late-1980s. "Delfts" removed. This mark appears on a wide variety of reproductions such as Blue Willow, Pink Luster, Imari, Flo Blue, etc. Appears in a wide variety of colors.

New   **Old**

The two marks, above left, were used on antique reproductions ca. 1970-1990s. Note that these two new marks do *not* include the letter "s" as the Delfts marks previously discussed. Both new marks are applied as backstamps. These particular new marks are somewhat similar to the genuine trademark, above right, of De Porceleyne Fles (Royal Delft) of Holland. This mark has the word Delft under a stylized vase. The backstamped Fles mark has been in use since 1879 to the present day. However, all old Fles marks also include an *impressed* date letter. In this example, the date letter is AK which represents the year 1915 (also see Royal Goedewaagen and Schoonhoen listings in this same chapter) .

New

Another new "Delfts" mark spelled with an "s" on the end. This mark is registered to the Blue Delft Co. of the USA. Used ca. 1990.

China and Porcelain

Doyen, Belgium

Unidentified importer's mark. Appearing as backstamp and foil labels on reproductions imported during the 1970s.

F–JS

This F-JS monogram is the mark of J. Finkelstein and Son, New York wholesalers and importers. The firm handled a wide range of products which includes many antique reproductions. The firm was apparently most active ca. 1960s-1980s.

Mark of J.Finkelstein & Son, right. Two reproduction urns in the European style from a ca. late 1970s catalog, far right.

Fiesta

The original line of Fiesta was made 1935-1973 by the Homer Laughlin China Co. In 1986, the company decided to put the pattern back in productions. It has been back in continuous production since that date.

Fiesta was so popular, many other china companies copied it. Fiesta collectors need to be able to separate not only genuine vintage

Typical authentic marks, 1935-1973

H.L.C.

fiesta
MADE IN
U.S.A.

fiesta
MADE IN
U.S.A.

fiesta
HLC USA

The main feature of 1935-1976 marks is the word "fiesta" in script with a lower case letter "f." The initials HLC, Made in USA and the Homer Laughlin monogram HLC, appear in various combinations. These marks appear as underglaze backstamps; simpler versions appear impressed (old impressed marks don't greatly differ from new impressed marks).

176

Fiesta marks, 1986–present

In 1986, the basic backstamp was changed to begin with an upper case "F."

The new Fiesta backstamp can include minor variations like the HLCO and USA in this example.

Slight changes continue to be made to the backstamp. This example was used in 2001.

Molded marks in new and old are substantially the same. This impressed mark used in 2002.

Fiesta from new Fiesta, but also separate genuine Fiesta from vintage imitators and look-alike patterns.

Unlike many brands of china, the great majority of authentic Fiesta–both vintage pieces and current wares–is marked. Pieces deliberately left unmarked are juice tumblers, demitasse cups and salt and pepper shakers. Other than these pieces, authentic Fiesta is always marked. Any unmarked piece offered as Fiesta without a mark should be viewed with caution.

Both new and old marks can be either an impressed mark formed in the mold or an inked backstamp. Molded marks have changed little

Homer Laughlin China Co. has kept this Spanish dancer trademark in constant registration since the 1930s. Vintage use was primarily for advertising and packaging.

China and Porcelain

between new and vintage production. If new pieces are made in old molds, new pieces will have the same marks as vintage pieces. Generally, all backstamps with a lower case "f" are 1935-1976 production. Fiesta with an upper case "F" has been used since 1986.

If in doubt about a mark, the best way to date authentic Fiesta pieces is by color and shapes. Colors of new production vary from original colors. Some shapes made now were never made in the 1935-1976 vintage period.

F–and crown

This is a modern fantasy mark found on reproductions of antique china. It was used ca. 1960 to mid-1980s. This example is green underglaze but probably in other colors as well. It is somewhat similar to genuine vintage marks on Furstenburg porcelain. Mark was probably created for an American importer.

Modern mark of F over crown Austria, left, is found on china reproductions like this transfer decorated portrait plate, right.

F–with crown

The modern mark of Michael Feinberg, Inc. registered 1990. It's somewhat similar to genuine vintage marks on Furstenburg porcelain.

178

Forest
Mark of Forest China Co., New York. Importer dealing in mostly ceramic goods including antique reproductions.

Fragonard
A facsimile signature on reproduction china. Usually found on portrait plates made 1970s-1990s. Usually appears somewhere in the decoration, not on the back.

Gainsborough
A facsimile signature on reproduction portrait plates made 1970s-1990s. The complete mark is "Gainsborough by John Peters, Amsterdam, Holland.

Gibson Staffordshire England
This mark was first registered in 1970. Another example of how the use of place names associated with antiques such as Staffordshire, cannot be used as your sole test of age.

Golden Crown
Although the mark includes the date 1886, this mark wasn't in use until the 1950s. It was used by Ebeling & Reuss Co., a Philadelphia importing firm.

CH Field Haviland
Current 1990s mark, registered to Jacque Jugeat, Inc.

179

China and Porcelain

H & Co

This is the mark of Heinrich & Co., Selb, Bavaria, Germany founded 1896. The firm is still in business. Generally, early marks do not include Heinrich at the bottom. Heinrich has been added to most marks ca. 1980s.

Current   **Old**

Hollohaza

Hollohaza is a trade name registered in the USA in 1990 by M & M Associates. It is found on handpainted ceramics including reproductions. The 1831 is not a date; actual country of origin is unknown.

Ironstone

Ironstone marks are listed in the chapter Blue Transfer Ware.

KB

KB in a shield is the mark of the New York importing firm of Koscherak Bros. used ca. 1920s-early 1980s. In the last 25 years, the firm carried extensive lines of antique reproductions made in Europe and later from Japan. Glass and china were specialities.

Backstamp and foil label of Koscherak Bros., NY.

KCI

Exact maker unknown. This mark is known to appear as a backstamp on reproduction ceramic shaving mugs.

180

Limoges

Although "Limoges" often appears in marks with the names of companies, Limoges is a geographic region in France, not a specific company. There are no legal restrictions on the use of Limoges and the word appears in many marks on reproductions to suggest age and quality. Limoges is often combined with other words and symbols that further suggest age including swords, shields, crowns, "artist signatures" and other images.

New
Gold backstamp, left, on reproduction plates including the one shown here. No old counterpart.

This Limoges mark in a banner with fleur-de-lis has been used on many reproductions since the 1960s. There is no old counterpart to this mark. The marks appear in colors of blue, green, red and black. Notice the banner includes the word "China," which no old mark ever did. This mark is found on many shapes including the covered box, top, and hatpin holder, right.

China and Porcelain

KPM

KPM is an abbreviation for the Königliche Porzellan Manufaktur (Royal Porcelain Manufactory) of Berlin. This operation, under various names, has produced porcelain from 1763 through the present day.

The high quality and famous marks of the original wares has made them frequent targets for imitators and forgers for years. Buyers need to be aware not only of current reproductions, but also the look-alike marks of the mid-19th and early 20th centuries. The following examples are only the most basic authentic marks and some typical imitations. There are many variations of each in the market.

Authentic KPM marks, 1840-WW I

Crowned Prussian eagle must include orb and scepter in talons. Stamped in blue underglaze, mid-19th century. The eagle always appears above the letters. Both the eagle and letters KPM are present in authentic marks. A scepter in the same color almost always accompanies the eagle. Line drawing of eagle only, left; photo of complete mark with scepter, right. Mid-19th century.

The scepter mark consists of a scepter above the letters KPM, line drawing, left. This mark is either impressed as shown here or in blue underglaze. Usually, plaques are marked with the impressed scepter mark. Mid-19th century.

Stamped blue underglaze, from 1911.

182

Confusing marks before 1925

KPM

Krister Porcelain,
ca. 1885.

KPF

Krister Porcelain,
(F not P), ca. 1903.

KPM / W

Krister Porcelain, ca. 1900.

K.P.M.

Kranichfield Porcelain, ca. 1903.

CHINA

KPM

Krister Porcelain,
ca. 1885.

Confusing marks after 1925

Krister Porcelain,
ca. 1885.

KPM
Krister
Germany

Royal
KPM
Porzellan

Kerafina,
1950-
1958.

K W M P

Krautzberger, Mayer & Purkett,
from ca. 1945.

Krister Porcelain Manufactory,
from ca. 1927

Modern reproductions

New demitasse cup and saucer sold by reproduction wholesaler in 1996 with faked KPM mark at right.

Fake KPM mark on new cup and saucer. This mark is cobalt blue transfer. Original mark included a scepter and was stamped, not a transfer.

Reproduction KPM-marked ceramic plaque sold by antique reproduction wholesalers in ca. 1970s-1980s. The reproduction is decorated with transfers. Vintage KPM is always hand-painted.

Lion–with wreath

New lion, crown and wreath fantasy mark, about two and one-quarter inches across. Appears in a variety of colors on many styles of reproductions including Flow Blue, Ironstone, Imari and many others.

The new lion mark appears on many reproductions including this new 18-inch platter. The multicolor turkey transfer is similar to several vintage patterns.

Mottahedeh

Mottahedeh & Company was founded by Mildred Mottahedeh in the 1970s. The business specializes in high quality ceramic reproductions of antiques. It often works with museums and other public collections to produce wares for sale in museum gift shops and for special fund-raising events. Manufacturing is contracted around the world, matching the job to the best qualified factory or studio.

Most, but not all, pieces are permanently marked. This can be the single word Mottahedeh or the name combined with a client's name. Edition numbers or other special marks may also be included.

Incised mark Motahedeh and edition number, 207/1000.

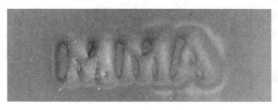
Reproduction majolica strawberry server made by Mottahedeh.

MMA–

The Metropolitan Museum of Art puts this mark on most, but not all, of the reproductions sold in the museum gift shop and catalog. This mark is impressed in a new piece of majolica made in the Philippines.

Similar MMA marks appear in other materials such as glass, metals, wood and paper. The nature of the mark depends on the material to which it is applied. See index for other examples.

185

China and Porcelain

PASCO

The mark PASCO was used by the Paul Straub Co., New York, from the late 1940s through at least the 1970s. Importers of giftwares particularly china and porcelain, including antique reproductions.

Old Foley–Olde Foley

A backstamp used by James Kent LTD, England, on reproductions of antique shapes such as toby jugs, shaving mugs and other 19th century shapes. Spelling varies slightly from mark to mark. Marks may or may not include England.

Old Foley-Staffordshire

Ye Olde Foley Ware

Old Foley

Trade names of Jame Kent pottery, England. These and marks with slight variations in spelling appear on ceramic reproductions like the scuttle shaving mug below.

Used in 1980-present. James Kent may appear in banner and Old Foley may appear in middle band.

186

N and crown

This backstamp was used on antique reproductions and giftwares imported into the USA ca.
1960-1980, possibly later. This example is red
but other colors probably also used.

There are a number of vintage marks which
include the letter N and a crown. The most
famous of these old marks is the N and crown of
18th century Capodimonte porcelain made in
Naples, Italy. The authentic
Capodimonte mark is hand
painted, not stamped or a transfer.

Crowns on early wares are
also quite different. Being hand
painted, early crowns are very
plain. Most prongs are single lines
or simple triangles formed in outline.

Transfer decorated "portrait" cup
and saucer with new N and crown
mark shown above.

Nippon

Japanese porcelain made for
export to the United States from 1891 to 1921 was marked "Nippon,"
not "Japan." In 1921, US officials ruled Nippon was a *Japanese* word
in violation of the McKinley Tariff Act which required the country of
origin to be an *English* word. Japanese ceramics imported into the
United States after 1921 are marked Japan, not Nippon.

For years, this knowledge was an easy rule of thumb collectors
used to their benefit. Any mark with Nippon had to be made before
1921 when the word was banned. This rule was generally true until the
1970s, when reproductions of porcelain marked Nippon began
appearing. By the late-1990s, reproduction importers were selling
new porcelain with marks virtually identical to marks found on genuine
pre-1921 originals.

The following marks point out the differences between new and
old. Keep in mind that reproduction importers are always improving
the quality of their fake marks. New marks closer to the originals can
appear at any time.

China and Porcelain

Genuine ca. 1891-1921 so-called wreath mark. Usually in a pale green transfer. Note the letter in the center is an upper case letter M.

Fake mark on reproductions introduced in 1997. A virtually exact copy of original. Pale green transfer.

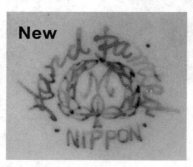

Fake mark introduced in 1996. It looks handpainted but it's a pale green transfer.

Another new mark introduced around 1996. Also looks handpainted, but it is also a pale green transfer.

The letter "K" rather than the letter "M" appears in the center of this fake mark first seen in 1993. A pale green transfer.

The earliest fake mark, ca. 1970 to 1980s. Hourglass rather than "M," in center, wreath upside-down.

Comparing wreath marks

New   **Old**

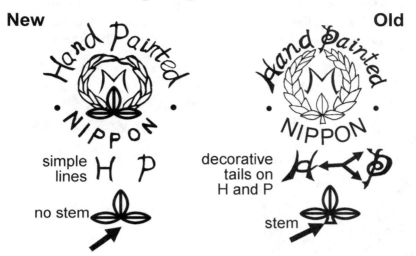

simple lines **H P**   decorative tails on H and P

no stem   stem

The letters "H" and "P" in Hand Painted on most new wreath marks are very plain, nearly simple straight lines. The triple-leaf cluster at the base of most new wreaths does not have a stem.

The letters "H" and "P" in Hand Painted on original marks are very ornamental. The lines goes from thick to thin and decorative flourishes at the ends. The triple-leaf cluster at the base of authentic wreaths has a clearly defined stem.

New RC mark is entirely green. RC is poorly formed, barely recognizable as English letters. Very weak outlines to letters.

In the old RC mark, "Hand Painted" is in red; "RC" and "Nippon" appear in green. Strong, distinct lettering (see color section for comparison).

China and Porcelain

There are several types of fake maple leaf marks found on reproductions. Some new marks do not include Nippon. In other new marks, the leaf is too large. The leaf in the original mark is only about one-quarter inch wide; leaves in new marks are one-half inch or more.

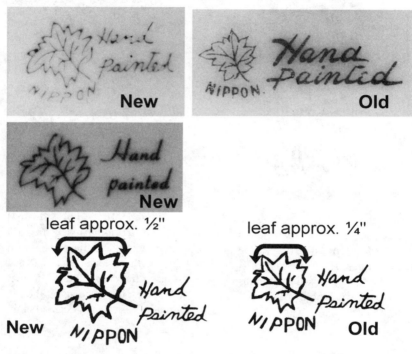

During WW I, the USA was cut off from porcelain blanks from Europe. Pickard and other American studios turned to Japanese blanks. One of the most recent fake marks is copied from one used by Picard on Noritake blanks imported during the war.

Fake mark, left, Hand Painted Nippon Ware, is now appearing in gold. The new mark is based on the original Pickard mark, right.

There are at least two different fake rising sun marks. New and old can be separated by the appearance of the rays and the sun's body.

New

Old

The body of the sun in the fake mark is shown in outline, not as a solid body.

In the original rising sun mark, the body of the sun is solid. Rays extending from the sun are solid spike-like rods.

New

First fake rising sun mark. There is a gap between the solid body of the sun and the jagged rays of the sun.

Fake plum blossom mark in pale green transfer. No known old counterpart.

Pickard China

Pickard is one of America's oldest continually operating china businesses. Although there were many marks used over the years, the two below are among the most frequently found. Although basically the same, there is a difference in the words that appear below the banner.

New

Current mark dating from the late-1980s.

Old

This mark used ca. 1938-1980s.

China and Porcelain

Quimper

Quimper is a generic term for pottery made in the city or region of Quimper, France. Major companies were HB Quimper, Porquier and Henriot Quimper (HR). Various mergers over the years have created many different modern marks.

VATOFEU
≫+B≫
QUIMPER
ca. late 1950s.

Henriot
Quimper
FRANCE
ca. 1974s.

Marks of Faiencerie de la Grander Maison, Quimper, France.

QUIMPER

Mark of Les Faienceries de Quimper, Quimper, France. This mark used ca. 1970-1984.

Mark of Quimper Faience Inc., Stonington, Connecticut. This company is located in Quimper, France, but owned by an American firm since 1984.

Railroad dining car china

Dining car china is a popular railroad collectible. So popular, it's been widely reproduced and reissued for a number of years.

Many new pieces are faithful recreations of original patterns and are fully marked and sold as reproductions. These pieces generally present little problem to collectors.

The bigger problem in railroad china comes from the unmarked

Dark blue mark on fake "Denver & Rio Grande" railroad china.

One of the new three-piece sets offered in the catalog page shown above. Colors of trademarks vary. Left to right: 2½-inch creamer; 3¼-inch butter; 2¾-inch mustard.

fantasy pieces mass produced by antique reproduction wholesalers. Such pieces typically have names of famous railroads like Union Pacific, New York Central, Santa Fe and others.

Your best defense against the cheaply made knockoffs is to keep in mind the purpose of original railroad china. All authentic railroad china had to withstand the constant shaking of rail travel, plus the usual demands of institutional china. That means authentic china is virtually without exception thick, strong and ruggedly made. All surfaces, except for some bottom rims, should be glazed. Many reproductions are intentionally highly glazed to imitate age.

New "railroad" china as shown on a catalog page from antique reproduction wholesaler. Clockwise from upper left: New York Central, Pennsylvania RR, Santa Fe, Union Pacific, Katy M-K-T, Missouri Pacific Lines. New, $5.50 per three-piece set .

China and Porcelain

New "D&RGRR" 3¾-inch cream pitcher and 2¼-inch egg cup. Note heavy blurring on egg cup.

Ridgway Potteries LTD

There have been various potteries using the name Ridgway for almost 200 years. Later companies may or may not have any connections to the original 19th century potteries. This particular mark is a backstamp in use from ca. 1960-1975.

Ridgway of Staffordshire England, EST 1792. This mark used only ca. 1960-1975.

Royal Carlton

This mark used ca. 1990 by New York importer, Arnart (see separate Arnart listing in this chapter).

ROYAL CARLTON

Royal Crown
Royal Crown Imperial
Royal Porcelain

These three marks are attributed to Arnart (see separate Arnart listing in this chapter) Importing. Exact dates not certain, but all are modern, ca. 1960-1980s at most.

ROYAL CROWN
ROYAL PORCELAIN

Royal Crown Imperial

Royal Vienna

This fantasy mark was used on antique reproductions made overseas, primarily Japan, for American antique reproduction wholesalers, ca. 1960-1980s.

Note the beehive orientation of the symbol originally used to represent a shield.

There are two companies whose names loosely translate into the English words of Royal Vienna–Wiener Porzellanfrabrik Augarten AG, ca. 1922 to the present, and KK Aerarial Porzellan-Manufactur Wien, ca. 1718-1864–and neither ever included "Royal Vienna," in English, in any mark.

Fantasy Royal Vienna "beehive" mark on reproductions from antique reproduction wholesalers. Blue backstamp.

The reproduction plates and other objects with this "Royal Vienna" mark are inexpensive transfer-decorated wares. Authentic pieces from either of the original companies are top quality porcelain with expertly handpainted decorations.

RS marks on china

Including RS Prussia, RS Germany, RS Suhl, RS Poland

Reinhold Schlegelmilch's initials, RS, appeared in various marks on fine German porcelain for almost 100 years, 1869 to 1956. Probably today's most desired pieces are those originally marked RS Prussia. Other sought-after marks include RS Germany, RS Suhl, and RS Poland.

RS Prussia marks have been widely forged and copied since the late-1960s. New RS Suhl marks appeared in the early 1990s, followed by fake RS Germany and RS Poland marked pieces in 1998.

Most original marks were applied fairly late in the production process. If protected at all, it was only with a light glazing; all RS marks are subject to wear. The basic authentic RS marks are the so-called wreath marks. Keep in mind there are *many other* authentic marks that include additional words and symbols. For our discussion, we are

Original RS wreath marks

ca.1870-1918 ca.1900-1917 ca.1912-1945 ca.1948-1956

Approximate dates the various authentic RS wreath marks were used on Schlegelmilch porcelain.

looking at only the wreath marks because they are the ones being reproduced.

There are several categories of new marks, including: 1) new marks on old but unmarked genuine RS pieces; 2) new marks on old porcelain from other manufacturers; 3) new marks on various kinds of new porcelain; and 4) mass-produced reproductions with close copies of old marks applied at the reproduction factory.

Individually applied fake and forged RS Prussia marks have been around since the late-1960s. New marks individually applied by do-it-yourself forgers frequently leave the surface surrounding these marks at different heights. Another good test is to use a long-wave black light, which can catch many attempts at reglazing the bottom to seal in a new mark.

New	Old

Reproduction 5-inch pitcher with faked RS Prussia wreath mark. The shape is a close copy of 19th century original shown at right.

This 5-inch pitcher is orignal mold #640. It was used as a model for the reproduction shown at left.

196

Checklist for RS Prussia marks

Use this chart to help identify typical new, fake, and forged RS Prussia marks.

	New	Old
"a" filled in, no period	**a**	**a.**
top does not extend to left	P	P
"i" not dotted	I	i
top of "R" not closed, thick/thin lines	R	R

Original RS Prussia marks, circa 1870 to 1918, have red letters, a red star, and red outlines to the wreath. Leaves in the wreath usually appear green. Red areas can look rusty brown; sometimes entire mark may be green.

Old

Red and green decal. Sold in sheets of 140 in late-1960s. Produced in America.

Red or green/blue ink stamp. "Prussia" not included. Since early 1980s on reproduction imports.

China and Porcelain

Red ink stamp. "Prussia" not included. From circa 1980 on reproduction imports.

Red and green transfer. Since early 1980s on reproduction imports.

Red and green transfer in current use (1998) on reproduction imports.

Handpainted forgery found on old but originally unmarked pieces.

Red and green transfer. "Prussia" not included. Ca. 1990 to present on reproduction imports.

Red and green transfer used since 1998 on reproduction imports.

New crude "RS Germany" mark, left, appears in blue-green paint. Original mark, right, is green or blue .

In the new mark, the letter "L" is uppercase with no period after it. The old Suhl has a lower case "l" and a period at the end. The letters, star, and outer edges of the wreath are red; the inside of the wreath is green.

New mark is handpainted in orange/red paint. Original mark is a transfer with the words "Made in (Germany) Poland" around the bottom. All lettering is red. This is the most recent of all the genuine RS marks. It was used after World War II, ca. 1948 to 1956.

China and Porcelain

RS

Unknown maker, probably from Japan. This mark appears on china reproductions 1980-1990s. Although the "Hand Painted" is included in the mark, all the examples I have examined have been transfer decorated, not painted.

Royal Staffordshire Pottery

The original mark was used by Arthur J. Wilkinson, ca. 1907. Vintage mark includes Burslem, England at the bottom of the mark. A virtually identical mark used from the 1970s has Wilkinson Ltd, England below the mark.

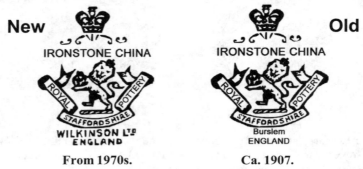

New   **Old**

IRONSTONE CHINA   IRONSTONE CHINA

WILKINSON Lᵗᵈ ENGLAND   Burslem ENGLAND

From 1970s.   Ca. 1907.

Royal Goedewaagen

This mark is registered to the Blue Delft Co. of the USA. Used ca. 1990. It appears on reproduction Delft.

Satsuma

This mark, "Hand-painted Satsuma," is stamped underglaze on crude reproductions of Nippon and Geisha Girl patterns. The removable paper labels are printed Made in China.

Backstamp on ceramic reproductions made in China.

Authentic Satsuma porcelain is a product of Japan. No vintage pieces ever included Satsuma spelled out in English.

Schoonhoven, Holland

This mark is registered to the Blue Delft Co. of the USA. Used ca. 1990. It appears on reproduction Delft.

J. Sonneville

Facsimile signature found on reproductions of new Delft. Signature is applied as a transfer, not handpainted. Probably on other ceramic reproductions as well.

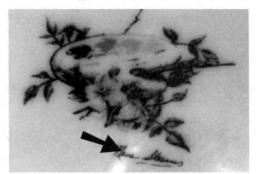

Neva Stevens

The mark of Neva Stevens as it appears on a new shaving mug. Excellent quality work and probably collectible for its own merits. Not to be confused with a vintage mark.

STW Bavaria

This mark is an American importer's mark found on reproduction china of the 1970s-1990s. The lettering and crown are black on a solid green shield. It is applied as a transfer. This mark may appear alone or with a blue stamped "beehive" as shown here. No old counterparts to this mark are known. It appears only on reproductions, 20 to 30 years old at most.

China and Porcelain

Wedgwood

Potters with the last name of Wedgwood have been in business in England since the 1700s. The most sought after work is that of Josiah Wedgwood and his sons. The basic marks of this firm are shown below, but there are many specialty marks as well.

Wedgwood shapes, styles, colors and techniques have been steadily copied for over 200 years. Most of the wares offered as "unmarked Wedgwood" or "Wedgwood style" are vintage copies or modern reproductions. Almost without exception, authentic Wedgwood is clearly and carefully marked. Many pieces of Wedgwood also have date letters, pattern ciphers and decorator marks which can pinpoint the exact year of production.

Authentic marks can be either impressed or printed depending on the specific mark. And while there can be considerable variation, there is one feature all authentic marks have in common–there is only one letter "e" in Wedgwood. If there is a letter "e" between the G and W, it is not an authentic mark.

WEDGWOOD
Basic all upper case mark used, ca. 1769-1891, either impressed or printed.

Wedgwood
Lower case mark, impressed, ca. 1780-1795.

WEDGWOOD
ENGLAND
The word England added to the basic mark in 1891, impressed or printed.

WEDGWOOD
Made in England
Made in England added to the basic mark ca. 1900, either impressed or printed.

WEDGWOOD
Wedgwood in sans serif uppercase letters first used 1929.

WEDGWOOD
Printed mark from 1878; so-called Portland vase mark.

WEDGWOOD
England
Printed mark from 1891.

WEDGWOOD
BONE CHINA
Made in England

Revised version of first Portland vase mark. Introduced in 1962. May have pattern names and numbers below.

★★★
WEDGWOOD
ENGLAND

Second Portland vase mark, from 1900. Note the three stars. Also appears with Made in England about 1910.

Printed mark used from 1940.

★★★
WEDGWOOD
BONE CHINA
MADE IN ENGLAND

Bone China added about 1920.

Weiss, Kuhnert & Co.

The German Doll Company, owned by American and German partners, has purchased an estimated 30,000 original molds used to make bisque figures during the late 19th and first third of the 20th century. A number of the old molds have been put back in production making new pieces that include original pre-1940 marks.

Subjects include bathing beauties, snowbabies, black figures, animals, half-dolls, character figures including Mickey Mouse and Kewpies, piano babies, santas, and figures in blimps, early airplanes and early autos. Shapes include jars, dolls, toothpick holders, vases, figures, holiday ornaments, doll heads and parts and a variety of other vintage shapes.

The great majority of the old molds came from the Weiss, Kuhnert

203

China and Porcelain

& Co. factory of Grafenthal, Germany. Weiss, Kuhnert began business in 1891. After WWII, the factory was nationalized by the East German communist government (German Democratic Republic). The firm continued to manufacture goods under various names through the postwar years but struggled after the fall of communism in the late 1980s and went out of business. The old molds are now being worked at the Walendorf Porcelain Factory where the new bisque is being made.

New bisque mermaid on alligator from original mold. Blond hair, handpainted features; 3" tall. Impressed mark, "Germany 7245" on back.

Since old molds are being used, many new pieces have the same old impressed marks found on vintage German bisque. Many of these marks include "Germany" plus a four digit number. The manufacturer, to its credit, does at least apply its new blue ink backstamp in the image of a toy. Unfortunately, the ink stamp is easily removed.

Impressed "Germany" and shape number, left, in new mermaid made from old mold is identical to the style of marks on vintage bathing beauties, right.

New bisque bathing beauties like the one at right are made in old molds. They often come packed in boxes with old-appearing marks like the example shown on the opposite page.

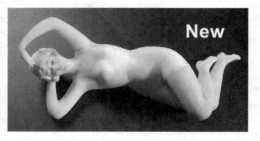

204

This is the mark of The German Doll Co. on most of the new bisque made from old molds. It appears as a blue ink stamp, actual size about three-eighths inch tall. It also appears in black ink on some packaging. This mark is easily removed.

Bottom view of new bisque piece made fromo old mold. Blue stamped mark on right and impressed "Germany" at arrow. Below, the ink stamped mark removed.

Some new bisque figures come in old cardboard boxes. This box, for example, has a Weiss, Kuhnert & Co. mark used during the 1970s (arrow).

Weiss, Kuhnert & Co. was nationalized in 1972 as Utility Porcelain VEB.

Marks of Wallendorf Porcelain Factory
Wallendorf, Germany

**VEB Wallendorf
Porcelain Factory
1958-59**

**VEB Wallendorf
Porcelain Factory
1960–**

WALLENDORF

**VEB Wallendorf
Porcelain Factory
1959–**

1764

**VEB Wallendorf
Porcelain Factory
1964–**

Wallendorfer

In 1976, the firm became a division of **VEB United Decorative Procelain works Lichte** in Lichte, Germany.

Marks of Weiss, Kuhnert & Co.,
Grafenthal, Germany

Weiss, Kuhnert & Co.
established 1891
Grafenthal, Germany,
ca. 1900-1956.

Weiss, Kuhnert & Co.
Grafenthal, Germany,
ca. 1956-1972.

Weiss, Kuhnert & Co.
was nationalized in 1972
as Utility Porcelain VEB.

NOTE: "VEB" represents Volkseigner Betreib or " People Owned Factory" and was the designation of factories nationalized under communist East Germany (German Democratic Republic) after World War II. VEB appears on many marks. No mark with VEB can be older than ca. 1946. Most marks with VEB date from 1950s or later.

Westward Ho

See Cowboy China listing in this same chapter.

Woods & Sons

Burslem, England. This mark used from 1970s. Note the phrase "Potters for 200 Years." Many English potters include the name "Woods" in their marks.

Ca. 1970s mark.

XOMEX

Incised mark XOMEX appears on the base of this new figural bulldog humidor. Originally includes Made in China paper label.

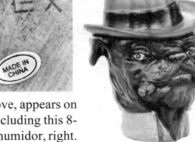

Incised mark XOMEX, above, appears on reproductions from China including this 8-inch figural bulldog humidor, right.

Zsolnay-Hungary

This mark registered to M & M Associates, ca. 1990. The date 1868 has no relationship to time of production. Two authentic marks shown for comparison.

New   **Old**   **Old**

Pottery

Pottery of all types has been one of the fastest growing fields of reproductions. Inexpensive foreign imports, as well as American-made fakes, have been increasing steadily since the mid-1990s.

There has been a disturbing trend to reregister genuinely old trademarks–such as McCoy and Bauer Pottery–with the U.S. Patent and Trademark Office. This gives present-day businesses the legal right to manufacture goods with marks virtually identical to those found on vintage pieces. When these pieces are bought on Internet auction sites or through other methods without a firsthand examination, it's easy to be fooled.

This chapter will show you some of the most recent pottery reproductions in the market today.

Three current reproductions of well-known originals. From top-center clockwise: Grueby-style tile, Etruscan Majolica sunflower pitcher, Little Red Riding Hood cookie jar.

Bauer Pottery

The "Bauer Pottery" name has been registered again and new pottery is being marked with various versions of the Bauer Pottery name. New products copy the so-called "ring ware" pieces originally manufactured in the 1930-40s using some of the original shapes as models. Los Angeles businessman Janek Boniecki registered the Bauer name in June, 1999.

New Bauer pottery. Left to right: 7½" bowl, 4" tumbler, 7" vase.

Boniecki's first products carried marks very similar to marks on original Bauer ring ware. Boniecki became aware his new products were being sold as originals and began adding "2000" to new Bauer Pottery in January 2000. However, many new pieces are in the market without the 2000 mark.

A good general rule to help separate new from old is that the vast majority of original Bauer has incised or impressed marks. Most, but not all, new Bauer has raised molded marks.

The original J.A. Bauer Pottery was located in Los Angeles, California. It produced utility goods, dinnerware and art pottery between 1910 and 1962. The original Bauer is perhaps best known for its dinnerware with molded rings similar to the Fiesta line by Homer Laughlin. Although the official Bauer name for the ringed line was California Pottery, most collectors refer to the line simply as "ring ware."

Raised new Bauer Pottery mark. All original Bauer marks are impressed, not raised.

Raised mark, new Bauer Pottery with 2000 added. Only some new pieces have the 2000 added.

Trademark of new Bauer Pottery as registered with U.S. Trademark and Patent Office.

Impressed version of new Bauer Pottery 2000 mark.

Paper label of new Bauer Pottery. Gold with black lettering with gray vase. Another version with a red vase is also used. Be alert for these new labels being removed and applied to all sorts of genuinely old, but unmarked, pottery of low value and being offered as vintage Bauer.

Exceptions to the rule about old marks being impressed. New Bauer Pottery impressed marks on new tumbler, left, and 8-inch flowerpot, right. Impressed marks without 2000 still appear on some pieces including the water pitcher.

Brush McCoy

See McCoy listing in this chapter.

Butterflies, flowers

There are no letters in this mark, only impressed butterflies. It was first seen in the mid-1990s on a number of different shapes including the strawberry pattern pitcher shown below. Unofficially attributed to a company under the name Ghent Pottery.

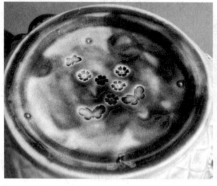 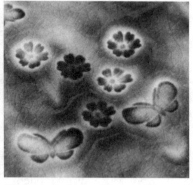

Impressed butterflies and flowers in the base of this new majolica pitcher by Ghent Pottery.

Close up view of butterflies and flowers. Note crazing in glaze.

New Ghent Pottery strawberry pattern pitcher has impressed butterflies and flowers in base.

Photos of Ghent Pottery courtesy Sam Pennington, Maine Antique Digest.

East Knoll Pottery

Contemporary handmade reproductions of American country pottery. Includes redware, brown slip and yellow ware.

EAST KNOLL POTTERY

TORRINGTON CT

Impressed mark of East Knoll Pottery. Marks are often filled with glaze and difficult to decipher. Mark measures about 1½-inches left-to-right.

New one-quart jug in yellow hand-thrown clay. Mocha decorated cobalt "seaweed" or "feather" pattern.

Pottery and Stoneware

EZ–Eva Zeisel

The letters EZ appear on reproductions of Red Wing dinnerware originally designed by Eva Zeisel. Zeisel's Town and Country pattern, created in the 1950s, has been reproduced by both the Metropolitan Museum of Art and Museum of Modern Art. Reproductions from the Metropolitan Museum are quite detailed and clearly state the piece is a "revival of a design" and cannot easily be confused with any vintage mark.

The EZ mark on Museum of Modern Art reproductions includes only the letters EZ and two digits, either 97 or 98. This mark does not provide the same clear warning as the more complete mark on the Metropolitan Museum's copies.

Reproduction Town and Country items from Museum of Modern Art are marked with either a EZ 98 or EZ 97 stamped in black ink.

A Revival of a 1947
design by
Eva Zeisel
© 1998 M M A
Made in Italy

The more complete mark used by Metropolitan Museum of Art on its reproductions of Town and Country.

Ephraim Faience Pottery

Ephraim Faience Pottery is a present-day pottery in Wisconsin specializing in reproductions of Arts and Crafts-styled pieces. It has used at least two impressed marks, which are shown here. Note that the word Faience does not appear in the second mark. Both marks are completely new forms; there is no old American pottery with any similar mark. Any piece with this mark can't be older than ca. 1990 at most.

The first Ephraim Faience Pottery mark which began appearing in late 1990s.

Known products include jardinieres, vases and a line of tiles. Most Ephraim products imitate patterns, colors and forms of original

Second mark of Ephraim Pottery, ca. 2002. The word Faience has been removed from the mark. Ephraim Pottery appears outside the circular symbol.

Arts and Crafts-era potters such as Newcomb College, Grueby and others.

Multicolored 8-inch Ephraim vase with incised oak-tree band around shoulder.

Ephraim multicolor 4-inch tile similar to Grueby originals

Four Rivers Stoneware

This is the backstamp of a Kentucky pottery that decorates some of its new pottery with patterns originally used by Watt Pottery. The backstamp appears in

green ink. Shapes are also copied from Watt original shapes. New Watt shapes and Watt patterns have been made by this operation since the mid-1990s.

Pottery and Stoneware

LN Fowler

LN Fowler of London, England, was a leading advocate of the use of phrenology—a 19th century study of contours and bumps in the human skull—to diagnose illness and personality disorders. Supplies of charts, books, diagrams and models related to phrenology were also sold by a firm founded by Fowler. Most products bear the name LN Fowler often with London, England.

Mark on side of new head, "LN Fowler, Ludgate Circus, London."

But just because pieces are marked LN Fowler doesn't mean they are old. New phrenology busts have been made with Fowler's name and often the word London since the mid-1990s. These reproductions are technically legal, as long as they are not marked Made in England. Most of the reproductions are made in China and Indonesia. These pieces are legally importable as long as they have removable paper labels declaring the country of origin.

A good way to separate most new from old ceramic pieces is to

New 12-inch head marked "Fowler," left, is a close copy of the original marked Fowler, right. The reproduction sells for between $35-$40; the original is worth $1,000-$1,500.

Base of new pottery phrenology head has large hole from slip casting. Bases of old pottery heads are solid, without large holes. Old pieces might have pencil-tip sized firing holes, but nothing like this 2-inch opening.

look at the bases. The vast majority of reproductions are made in slip molds, a process which leaves a large, nearly perfectly circular hole. Bases of originals are solid, without holes.

Fulper Pottery

Fulper Pottery of Flemington, New Jersey was started in the early 1800s but is best known for its Arts and Crafts-styled art pottery produced between 1909 and 1930. In 1930, former Fulper superintendent J. Martin Stangl bought Fulper Pottery and shifted the emphasis from art pottery to other wares.

The Fulper name was revived in 1984 by four granddaughters of William Hill Fulper II, who started Fulper Glazes, Inc. The new Fulper began making products very similar to 1909 to 1930s originals, with glazes said to be made from original formulas. Among the new

New multicolored tile issed by the new Fulper Glazes, Inc.

New lamp base by Fulper Glazes, Inc. Glaze is similar to vintage Fulper glaze.

215

Pottery and Stoneware

New
Mark of modern Fulper Glazes, Inc. with right angled corners and word "Tile."

Original
Fulper Pottery marks are enclosed by rounded border.

products are lamps and tiles made famous by the original Fulper Pottery.

The new wares can be separated by the embossed mark "Fulper Tile" set in two square-cornered boxes. Marks of the original Fulper never include the word "Tile."

Grueby

A faked ink stamp Grueby pottery mark started showing up in early 2000. The mark is rubber stamped in dark blue ink and covered with a new glaze.

The fake "Grueby Faience Co. Boston, U.S.A." mark is a copy of an old original mark. A similar original mark reads "Grueby Pottery Boston, U.S.A." Both authentic lotus marks are *impressed* in the clay, not ink stamped.

Fake "Grueby Faience" blue ink stamp
Terry Stern photo

Authentic Grueby Faience lotus mark; always impressed, never ink stamped.

Authentic Grueby Pottery lotus mark; always impressed, never ink stamped.

Hull Pottery

Reproductions of Hull Pottery are being seen in Orchid and Bow-Knot. So far, both patterns are made here in the United States. New pieces have marks very similar to original markings.

Many pieces of Hull Little Red Riding Hood have also been reproduced. Several of those pieces, like the cookie jar, have marks identical to the old originals. Hull sold Little Red Riding Hood products between 1943 and 1957.

Hull contracted the decorating and production of blanks for most Red Riding Hood Products to Royal China and Novelty Co., a part of Regal China. The basic design for original Little Red Riding Hood pottery was created by Louise Bauer. Bauer received U.S. patent

New Orchid vase, left, closely resembles original, right. There are differences in the marks (see comparison of marks).

Mark on new Hull Orchid vase. Note the script style of lettering, which is particularly evident in the word Hull. Also note that the size in the mark is "10¼."

Mark on original Hull Orchid vase. Note that the lettering is a block style, not script like the reproduction mark on left. Note the size in the mark is 10¾, not 10¼.

Pottery and Stoneware

number 135,889 for her design June 29, 1943. The patent was then assigned to Hull Pottery. Although many original pieces of Little Red Riding Hood are marked with the patent number, the Hull name or some combination of the two, many original pieces are unmarked. Reproductions almost always include some imitation of original marks.

Some reproductions of shapes originally made by Hull are marked "McCoy." Those pieces are covered under the McCoy listing in this chapter.

Because so many Hull marks are included on reproductions, size and quality are generally much better tests of age than marks.

Mark on new Hull Bow Knot cornucopia, "U.S.A. Hull Art B-5-7½," the same as the original. Image blurred due to thick glaze.

Impressed mark on new Hull cookie jar is the same as the mark that appears on the original.

New Hull Little Red Riding Hood cookie jar. This new jar has exactly the same mark as original Hull Little Red Riding Hood jars.

Original Hull Little Red Riding Hood cookie jar. This jar has the same mark as the reproduction.

218

The best way to separate new and old Little Red Riding Hood cookie jars marked Hull is by size. Reproductions are 12-inches tall; original jars are over one-inch taller at 13¼-inches.

Old

967
Little Hull Ware
Red Riding Hood
Patent Applied For
U.S.A.

Impressed mark on original Hull cookie jar, left, shown as line drawing for clarity. The new and old marks are the same.

Old

Pat-Des-No-135889
U.S.A.

Hull Ware
U.S.A.

Little Red Riding Hood
Pat-Des-No-135889
U.S.A.

Three other authentic marks which may appear on authentic Hull Little Red Riding Hood pieces. These marks are all impressed below the surface. Marks on reproductions are often raised because it is easier to cut the molds to produce raised marks.

Pottery and Stoneware

McCoy

The Nelson McCoy Pottery has roots going back to the 1890s. One of its most widely used marks was simply McCoy in raised letters. Unfortunately, trademark registration for this original McCoy mark was allowed to lapse.

In 1991, the mark was registered again by a person in Tennessee. The mark has since been used on a wide variety of reproduction pottery. The new pottery includes a raised "McCoy" mark identical to the vintage McCoy mark.

The new McCoy mark appears not only on reproductions of original McCoy pottery, but pottery made by other collectible vintage makers such as Hull, Shawnee and other manufacturers.

You cannot use the McCoy mark as a test of age. Compare the pattern and shape of a suspected piece to confirm they were originally made by McCoy and not another pottery.

McCoy mark appearing on many pieces of vintage McCoy.

Reproduction Red Riding Hood cookie jar, left, is marked "Mc-Coy" on the base in raised molded letters, right. The mark is identical to an original McCoy mark. However, no Red Riding Hood cookie jars were ever made by McCoy. Vintage Red Riding Hood cookie jars were made by Hull Pottery, not McCoy.

McCoy–Brush McCoy

The original Brush-McCoy Pottery operated ca. 1911-1925. It was formed by members of the McCoy family and George Brush, who owned a small pottery. The new firm was called Brush-McCoy, with Brush as general manager. The McCoys left the company in 1925, leaving George Brush the entire operation. The business was renamed Brush Pottery to reflect his sole ownership.

Brush Pottery is credited with being among the first American potteries to produce cookie jars, introducing its first in 1929. Brush joined other potters in making figural cookie jars in the mid-1940s. The company closed in 1982.

Some of the most desirable of the original Brush Pottery cookie jars were designed by Ross and Don Winton of Twin Winton Ceramics. Most Brush Pottery cookie jars designed by the Wintons are marked with a large W.

As a general rule, most but far from all, authentic Brush Pottery marks are incised or impressed below the surface.

There has been a confusing fantasy mark on reproductions of Brush Pottery cookie jars appearing at least since 2001 and maybe

Fantasy "Brush McCoy" mark with paintbrush and "W-8," left, appears on this reproduction of a Brush Pottery cookie jar. The reproduction, right, is known as Elephant with Ice Cream Cone. The original was made by Brush Pottery in the early 1950s.

New "Brush McCoy" mark, left, in raised molded letters as it appears on the Mugsy reproduction jar, right. Original Mugsy cookie jars were made by Shawnee Pottery, not Brush Pottery.

earlier. The new mark includes the words "Brush McCoy" separated by a paint brush. A number of the new marks add to the confusion by including a large letter W similar to the Winton W which appears in authentic marks.

There is no old counterpart to the Brush-McCoy mark. All such marks are new. The original Brush-McCoy pottery, ca. 1911-1925, never made any decorative high-glazed cookie jars. Neither did it ever use a similar mark. Collectible cookie jars were made by Brush Pottery ca. 1929-1982, not Brush-McCoy.

The new mark also appears on reproductions of patterns and shapes originally made by other potteries. A Mugsy cookie jar, for example, shown here, was originally made by Shawnee Pottery. This Mugsy reproduction is marked "Brush McCoy" on the base.

Close up view of fantasy "Brush McCoy" raised molded mark. Brush and McCoy separated by molded paintbrush. No old counterpart to this mark.

Two typical marks of Brush Pottery that appear on that company's cookie jars, ca. 1940s-1982. The W represents those jars designed by Twin Winton Ceramics. The closest original mark to include a paintbrush was the palette mark, right. Most original marks were impressed or incised, not raised.

So far, all the new Brush McCoy pottery marks have been in raised molded letters. This is unlike most original Brush Pottery marks, shown above, which are generally, but not always, incised or impressed.

MW–Majolica Wares

A modern company specializing in reproductions of Victorian majolica. Many, but not all, of its products have the letters MW incised

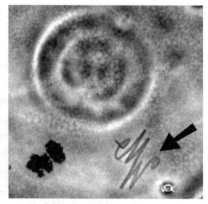

New sunflower pattern water pitcher by Majolica Works copied from an original pitcher marked "Etruscan Majolica." The new pitcher includes the old mark.

The new "Etruscan Majolica" mark as it appears on the bottom of new MW sunflower pitcher. Don't mistake the incised MW (arrow) for a decorators mark and think the piece is old.

Pottery and Stoneware

Above left, incised MW mark on the back of this new cauliflower pattern plate, right. Penny included for size comparison of mark. The cauliflower pattern was originally made by Etruscan Majolica.

by hand into the bases. But a number of its new products also have original marks. The old marks are copied when new molds are taken from originals. New pieces made in the new molds will have copies of the old marks.

Although the new Etruscan example shown here is blurred, it is not much worse than many old marks which are frequently filled in with glaze and hard to read. The old Etruscan mark shown for comparison is particularly sharp and clear. Many old marks aren't much sharper than the new copy.

Most of the MW products are copied from specific well known patterns by famous makers from the United States. These include Etruscan patterns in cauliflower and sunflower, figural pieces originally by George Jones and copies of Minton.

The great majority of new majolica is produced by slip casting. This leaves holes where handles join pitcher bodies and most knobs join lids. Most old handles and knobs were made as separate solid pieces

An exceptionally sharp original Etruscan Majolica mark.

224

and joined to pitcher bodies and lids.

Mucha

Alphonse Mucha was an important artist and designer of the Art Nouveau period. Exact copies of his work with his name and dates have appeared on new ceramic tiles made in England since the mid-1990s. The new tiles are exact copies of Mucha's work that appeared on original tiles ca. 1880-1910.

New 6-inch tile signed "Mucha." Based on original titled *Le Lierre* (Ivy) of 1901.

Since new tiles are based on original designs and patterns, being familiar with old designs is of little help in identifying the new tile. A more reliable test is to look for clues of modern color printing used to prepare the new transfers. Transfers applied to the new tiles are printed using modern color printing. Vintage transfers were lithographed and do not have this pattern.

Typical "Mucha" facsimile signature and date that appear on new tile. Exact signature and dates vary.

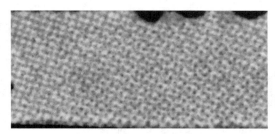

Regular dot pattern characteristic of modern color process printing. Old transfers do not show this pattern.

Pottery and Stoneware

North Prairie Tileworks

A rubber stamped mark in black ink found on reproduction pottery tiles; possibly appears on other pottery forms as well. The sample mark shown here appears on a reproduction of a Rookwood tile. There is no old counterpart to this company name.

Rubber-stamped North Prairie Tileworks mark, above, is on the back of this reproduction Rookwood tile, right.

Painter Pottery Works

Wyn Painter is a present-day potter specializing in commemorative stoneware. A sample two-inch brown and white jug with blue lettering is shown here. All of Painter's new pieces are clearly marked with his name, but not necessarily dated.

New sample stoneware jug by Kansas City potter Wyn Painter to promote his commemorative stoneware business. Painter marks all of his new stoneware with his name to avoid confusion with antique pieces. Front of jug, above left; reverse of jug, upper right; base of jug, below.

Backstamp on bottom of one of WA Painter's stoneware jugs.

Phaidon, Phaidon Group

A tabletop and gift accessory company whose line includes majolica reproductions. Mark can be Phaidon or Phaidon Group. The mark may or may not include a date. This particular mark was found on the blackberry pattern teapot shown here.

Phaidon Group mark, left. This example includes the registration symbol, ®, and the copyright symbol, ©. The blurred date is 1988, not 1888. The mark appears on the blackberry pattern teapot, right.

Red Wing Stoneware Company

The new Red Wing Stoneware Company (RWSC) is not a descendant of the original pottery of the same name. The current

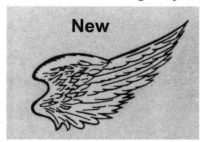

New wings are made of crisp solid lines.

Old wings almost always show smudges and feathering of lines.

227

Pottery and Stoneware

RWSC was gradually brought to production during the mid-1980s. According to production manager Bill Israel, RWSC uses the same techniques today as earlier Red Wing potteries. "We use slip cast, wheel thrown and ram mold," said Israel. "Depending on size, we can put out 200-300 pieces of slip cast, up to 125 pieces of wheel thrown and 100-200 pieces of ram-molded products per day." Clay for the stoneware comes from Roseville, Ohio.

RWSC currently produces many shapes similar to those collectors associate with late 19th and early 20th century production. These include bean pots, pantry jars, preserve jars, covered bowls, pitchers and crocks. Decorations include spongeware and molded designs like cherry bands.

New

Old

New oval mark, blue lettering. No original pre-1900 Red Wing Stoneware Company mark was stamped in blue ink in an oval.

Blue oval mark of Red Wing Union Stone ware Company. This is the original mark that appeared with the red wing, ca. 1906-1930s.

New

Old

Left, new two-gallon crock made today by Red Wing Stoneware Co. of Red Wing, MN. A two-gallon crock made by Red Wing Union Stoneware Co, of Red Wing, MN, ca. 1906-1930.

New    **Old**

Dark blue stamp on new Red Wing Stoneware Company pieces.

The only original stamp used 1906-1930s with the company name spelled out.

Registry marks

The diamond-shaped British Registry marks were used beween 1842 and 1883. Different letter and numbers in the various sections recorded the year of manufacture and other facts helpful to collectors.

Reproduction importers have used raised molded, but blank, Registry-shaped diamonds on a variety of pottery to suggest age. The diamond shapes are conveniently "filled in" with glaze or paint.

These marks have been found on copper luster pieces, blue and white parian-style wares and ironstone. In April 2002, Connie Swaim of *Antique Week* reported a piece of new majolica was found with a similar registry-style mark.

Since Registry marks were required by British law, all such marks had to be legible. Any mark represented as a British Registry diamond that does not clearly have relatively clear and legible letters and numbers is virtually certain to be a forgery.

Illustration of a molded Registry diamond on reproductions. All fields are blank as if filled in by glaze or paint.

Authentic molded British Registry diamond with proper fields. Original molded Registry marks are relatively legible.

Pottery and Stoneware

Rookwood Pottery

There are two types of new Rookwood circulating in today's market. The first group consists of unauthorized fakes and copies having no connection to the original company. These pieces are usually individually made to intentionally deceive or are made in limited numbers in imitation of original patterns and shapes. The other pieces are from the "new" Rookwood Pottery operating again in Cincinnati, Ohio, with molds rescued from the original Rookwood company.

The original Rookwood Pottery was founded in Cincinnati, Ohio, in 1880. For 50 years, its products were considered some of the world's finest art pottery. Then the Great Depression and shortages of material in World War II led to the company's failing. The company passed through various owners and shut down completely in 1967.

The molds and equipment were in storage through 1982. That's when Arthur Townley, a Michigan dentist, made a deal to buy everything that remained. It included the molds and the Rookwood name with all its trademarks including the reverse R and P with flames.

Townley began making pieces from original molds in the mid-1980s. The new Rookwood has the same RP flame mark as the original, but there are several major differences. First, all the new pieces are dated in *Arabic* numbers, not Roman numerals. The dates are *ground into the glaze* with a diamond drill, not cast into the ceramic material. New Rookwood is all stark white *porcelain,* not the softer Ohio clay used in the original pottery.

Individually forged marks are hard to categorize due to their one-

New Rookwood has the impressed "RP" and flames mark with the year of production *engraved* in *Arabic* numerals, not Roman numerals.

Original impressed RP and flames mark. The year of production is in *Roman* numerals. The year shown is 1920.

of-a-kind nature. As a general rule, authentic RP and flames mark must always be accompanied by a model number. Another good indication of an authentic mark is to look for the small "hooks" that appear on the ends of authentic flames surrounding the RP. Most faked marks don't include this small detail. Original Roman numeral year dates are about one-third the size of the RP and flames. Roman numerals on the fakes are frequently much larger or much smaller than original year dates

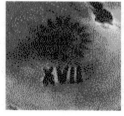 Fake  Old

Close-up of forged Rookwood mark. Roman numerals too large, no hook to tips of flames, no model number.

Authentic mark. Note hooks on flame tips. Mark includes model number 1222.

Roseville Pottery

The original Roseville Pottery Co. was founded in 1892 in Roseville, Ohio. In 1898, the pottery relocated to Zanesville, Ohio, where all the art pottery was made. The business closed in 1954.

The first commercially made reproductions of Roseville Pottery from China began appearing in late 1996. Most reproductions are from the Late Period. Marks on Late Period reproductions fall into two groups: Group A is marked exactly the same as originals; Group B is marked nearly the same as originals. All original Late Period pieces

Left, Group A mark on new Magnolia vase includes raised "Roseville, USA," shape code "90," and size number "7." New mark identical to original mark, right, found on authentic 7-inch Magnolia vases.

231

were marked on the base in raised letters, "Roseville U.S.A.," followed by a shape code and size number. The only exceptions are a very few creamers, sugars, flower frogs, candle holders, and other small pieces where part of the mark is omitted for lack of space. Group A reproductions are marked exactly like originals with the raised "Roseville, U.S.A.," shape number, and size.

However, U.S. Customs ruled that "U.S.A." in the reproduction mark implied the reproductions were made in the United States. Chinese manufacturers were ordered to remove it, and marks on the next wave of reproductions, Group B reproductions no longer include the raised "U.S.A."

All letters of original Late Period raised marks–"Roseville, U.S.A.," shape code, and size number–are an equal height above the surface. Some Group B marks are still found with a very faint or very unevenly formed "U.S.A." If you find "U.S.A." in weak, shallow letters but with Roseville and shape numbers sharp and clear, it is from a new mold where the "U.S.A." has not been completely removed. The absence of the "U.S.A." is now an important clue to the detection of the Group B reproductions.

Original Middle Period patterns–Luffa and Jonquil for example–are virtually never found with a permanent mark. The vast majority was marked with paper labels only. When an authentic Middle Period piece is found with a permanent mark, it is the single word "Roseville" only, incised or impressed below the surface of the clay. Chinese reproductions of Luffa and Jonquil are permanently marked with the single word "Roseville" in *raised* letters. This is the exact opposite of the incised or impressed authentic mark found on originals of the same pattern.

Left, new Group B mark with "U.S.A." very faint. Except for a handful of very small original shapes, "U.S.A." is the same height as all other raised lettering in authentic Late Period Roseville raised marks.

Roseville copies have also been made on a more limited scale in the United States. Many of the American-made fakes have "Rv" marks stamped in ink. Fake-ink stamped marks of "Roseville Rozane" have also been found in blue ink under new glaze.

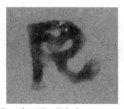

Fake Crude "Rv" ink stamp in light blue. Original ink stamp marks are deep navy blue, almost black.

Fake Poorly formed and watery "Rv" ink stamp in very pale blue.

New Raised script mark appears on Chinese reproductions of Middle Period patterns such as Luffa and Jonquil. No original Middle Period patterns ever had such a raised script mark.

This American-made reproduction has the Middle Period script mark correctly incised.

RRPCO

Robinson Ramsbottom Pottery Co. of Roseville, Ohio–whose mark is R.R.P. Co– is frequently confused with the Roseville Pottery Company of Zanesville, Ohio.

While Roseville Pottery has a number of different marks, Robinson Ramsbottom Pottery has only slight variations of the uppercase letters RRPCO. Most marks are impressed or incised.

With the exception of some cookie jars made 1935 through the

Pottery and Stoneware

1960s, most Robinson Ramsbottom pottery is utilitarian and not particularly collectible. It continues in operation today.

R.R.P.CO
ROSEVILLE OHIO

The standard mark of Robinson Ramsbottom Pottery Company of Roseville, Ohio, generally incised or impressed. There is no connection between this company and Roseville Pottery of Zanesville, Ohio.

Shawnee Pottery

There are various reproductions of Shawnee Pottery. A number of Shawnee cookie jars have been reproduced but those are usually marked "McCoy" or "Brush McCoy." They are covered under the McCoy listing in this same chapter (also see index). New pieces with the Shawnee include reproductions of Shawnee's Corn King and Corn Queen pieces and new foil labels which can appear on a number of pieces.

Reproduction #73 Shawnee corn ware casserole, left; original on right. These and similar pieces began appearing in the mid-1990s.

Bottom of reproduction #73 corn ware casserole has the same raised mark as the original Shawnee #73 covered dish.

Bottom of original #73 casserole. Note original standing rim (arrows) is *unglazed*; rim on fake is glazed.

The new corn ware pieces are marked exactly the same as the originals, with the mark in raised lettering on the bases. The key difference between new and old is that the standing rim, or table rim, is glazed in new bases; it is unglazed on old bases. There have been a number of new corn pieces reported including the #70 creamer.

New foil labels have been used on new pottery sold as new collectibles by an individual in Ohio since 1994. Although the new products are probably collectible for their own merits, the new labels may create confusion when placed on other pieces, especially when foil labels were often used on vintage Shawnee pieces.

The key difference in separating vintage from new labels is whether the label has a tomahawk or arrowhead. Vintage labels include an arrowhead; new labels have a tomahawk.

New

New labels include a tomahawk on the left side of the label.

Old

Original labels have an arrowhead on the left side of the label.

Pottery and Stoneware

Treasure Craft

Treasure Craft is a present-day comany reproducing vintage collectible cookie jars. Most jars are made in China and enter the U.S. with a removable Made In China paper label. Marks are impressed on bases.

©Treasure Craft

Impressed mark of Treasure Craft, a company reproducing vintage cookie jars.

The original Cow Jumped Over Moon cookie jar was made by Robinson Ramsbottom Pottery Co. and that company's mark appears on the original. A reproduction of the same jar, right, is made by Treasure Craft, whose name is marked on the base.

Mickey and Minnie Turnabout

The old Mickey and Minnie Turnabout cookie jar was marketed by Leeds China Company of Chicago, Illinois. Leeds had a license to sell Disney related character merchandise from 1944 to 1954. Included among its products were figural cookie jars of Dumbo, Pluto, Donald Duck, Joe Carioca, Mickey and Minnie, and others. Leeds was a distributor only, not a pottery manufacturer. The jars were primarily made at Ludowici Celadon Company of New Lexington, Ohio, but also by American Bisque and other companies.

New Mickey/Minnie Turnabout cookie jar

One of Leeds' special features was its "Turnabout" jars. These jars showed a different character or view on the reverse side than what was on the front. Mickey on one side, for example, and Minnie on the other. Similar Turnabouts have Pluto/Dumbo, Donald Duck/ Joe Carioca, and a double sided Dumbo.

Marks on the original Turnabouts are in raised molded letters like

236

the new mark shown below from the new Mickey/Minnie Turnabout. As you can see, there are two glaring spelling mistakes. Mickey is spelled "MICKY" and patented is spelled "PATENDED."

There is also the measuring tape test. The original jar is 14½", two inches taller the copy which is only 12½" high. This is obvious when new and old are side by side, but not so apparent when the pieces are separated unless you measure.

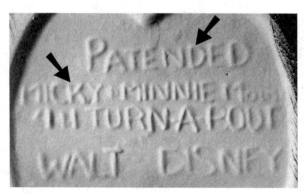

Raised molded mark on bottom of new jar. Note the misspelling in "PATENDED," top arrow, and MICKY, bottom arrow. Correct spelling is PATENTED and MICKEY.

Van Briggle Pottery

Van Briggle Pottery was founded by Artus Van Briggle in 1901 in Colorado Springs, Colorado. After Artus died in 1904, the pottery was managed by his wife Anna, who ran the business until about 1912.

Various managers and owners then operated the pottery through the 1920s. In 1931, the name was changed back to Van Briggle Art Pottery, which remains in active production to this day.

Collectors need to be aware of the marks appearing on new Van Briggle made today, as well as forged marks on fakes and reproductions.

Despite the various business names of the pottery over the years, words and symbols in genuine Van

This butterfly bowl has been in almost constant production with similar marks since 1907.

Briggle marks have been fairly consistent. Authentic marks fall into two broad categories: marks used 1901 to 1920; and marks after 1920. The vast majority of authentic marks from both periods include a monogram of back-to-back letter As and "Van Briggle." Pre-1920 marks usually included a date and often had a design or glaze number. After 1920, pieces were rarely dated and Colorado Springs was added, usually abbreviated as "Colo Spgs." There is considerable variation among authentic marks because marks were inscribed by hand, rather than molded or stamped.

At this time, there is no single test or clue to catch the fakes. Many forged marks are virtually identical to original marks. Generally, you should be wary of any unusually rough or crude marks. Be especially suspicious of flat sided, trench-like lines or grooves in marks. Such marks may have been engraved with rotary tools after the clay has been fired. Also be wary of any marks with the clay raised along the lines of the mark.

As for marks on new pieces made today at Van Briggle, they are virtually the same as marks that appear on vintage pieces made from the 1930s on. Therefore, marks alone are not a reliable test of age for any post-1930 pieces. The only practical way to date many of these pieces is by carefully comparing which glazes appeared on which during what years. Always insist that a written receipt for Van Briggle include the approximate date of production.

Typical marks in use today at Van Briggle Pottery

Typical mark used on new Van Briggle Pottery is similar to marks on vintage pieces.

There is no question about the age of this mark. The ink-stamped VB 100 definitely never appeared on a vintage piece.

CO. upper left, purpose unknown. COLO. SPRINGS on one line. VAN BRIGGLE all upper case. Initials RJT and 11 or II in bottom.

VAN BRIGGLE all upper case. COLO SPGS Colo abbreviated without punctuation. Initials C-P at bottom.

A piece thrown after the day's regular work, marked ORIGINAL. Initials BWL at the bottom.

IV, 2 top. VAN BRIGGLE and COLO. SPRINGS upper case. Colorado abbreviated CO. RJT at bottom.

*Van Briggle illustrations
courtesy Ron Lindsey*

IV upper right; I. S. and 2 attributed to finisher's marks, bottom. Script Van Briggle on two lines. COLO SPGS upper case.

VAN BRIGGLE all upper case, as is COL. SPRGS. Note that an additional "R" is added to SPRGS. V, 11 or II and BWL at bottom.

239

Typical fake and forged Van Briggle marks

Forged mark with finisher initials "AO." The forged initial "O" does not match the "O" found in original marks. The original O has a loop in the upper right.

New   **Old**

William Schluze photo

Fake mark showing finisher number "28" and finisher initials "AO." Two different finisher marks never appear on the bottom of an original.

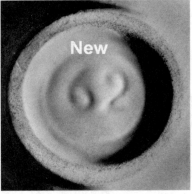

William Schluze photo

Watt Pottery

Watt Pottery reproductions with marks like original Watt have been produced since the early 1990s. Among new pieces with

Reproduction Watt Pottery mark on new #15 pitcher is virtually identical to mark on original #15 pitcher.

New mark on reproduction #62 Watt Pottery creamer. An almost exact copy of original mark.

imitations of old marks are the #15 pitcher and #62 creamer.

The easiest way to separate new from old Watt pitchers is to examine the area where handles meet the body. In new Watt Pottery pitchers, there is a definite dimple where handles meet the side wall of the body. The same area in original pitchers is smooth with no dimple.

New Watt pitchers have a dimple where the handle joins the body. This new pitcher has an identical copy of an original mark.

Original Watt pitchers are perfectly smooth where the handle joins the body.

Western Stoneware Company

A fake Sleepy Eye pottery paperweight marked "Western Stoneware Company" has been in circulation since the mid-to-late 1980s. The fakes exist in gray pottery and reddish-brown pottery. No old counterpart like the paperweight ever existed.

The original Western Stoneware Co. of Monmouth, Illinois, made a number of stoneware premiums for the original Old Sleepy Eye Flour Co., Sleepy Eye, Minnesota. (See index listings under Old Sleepy Eye for other fakes.)

Bottom of new paperweight marked WSWCO (Western Stoneware Co) Monmouth IL. Top of 2½-inch paperweight has Old Sleepy Eye.

Silver and Silverplate

Marks on precious metals have been regulated by law since ancient times. From pharaohs, Roman emperors and continuing today, fineness, or standard marks, have been used to guarantee minimum amounts of precious metal in relation to non-precious metal.

At least that's the theory. But while most governments strictly monitor standard marks, very few regulate marks not related to the content of precious metals. It is perfectly legal, for example, to stamp silver with trademarks or brand names of companies no longer in business or whose trademark is no longer registered. A new piece marked "Unger Bros."–a 19th century firm known for quality silver–and 925 is legal, as long as the silver content tests at 925.

Sterling and Silverplate

This presents obvious problems for those interested in antique and collectible silver and silverplate. This chapter will review some of the most common new and confusing marks appearing on 925/1000 silver and silverplate. Almost all the pieces we'll be discussing are made for the antique reproduction trade. The article will not include elaborate forgeries of museum-quality silver made before 1850 or silver of other standards. We will focus on the marks found on reproductions of small decorative and novelty pieces such as match safes, sewing accessories, pill boxes, chatelaines, thimbles and similar wares.

American silver marks

In America, articles marked sterling must contain a minimum of 925 parts silver for every 1000 parts of material. Expressed another way, items must be 92.5 percent silver and no more than 7.5 percent base metal. This ratio is called the "sterling standard" and has been used in the U.S. since the mid-1860s. The numeric 925 is the millesimal expression of the 925/1000 standard.

By far, the vast majority of qualifying items made in the U.S. ca. 1860 to 1970–especially items made before 1940–are marked "sterling" or "sterling silver." Many vintage marks, but far from all, include the name of the manufacturer. Very rarely are qualifying pieces of American silver from those years marked only "925." Rarer still, are American marks which include "sterling" and "925" together without a company name.

This doesn't mean all pieces marked sterling or sterling silver are old. But it is a general rule that virtually all pieces marked only "925" or "sterling" and "925" are modern.

The globalization of commerce has prompted nations to use the same units of weight, measure and standards to increase trade. In 1973, the European Community (EC) agreed to recognize 925/1000 as the official sterling silver standard and 925 as the official standard mark. Since then, almost all silver of that quality sold among EC member countries has the 925 standard mark. New silver marked 925 is also acceptable in the US because that is also the US standard.

In fact, the vast majority of mass-produced silver reproductions today, whether made in Thailand, India, England, Europe or America, now include 925 in the mark. With the 925 standard mark, a piece of silver can virtually be sold world wide with the

Silver and Silverplate

same mark.

The use of 925, however, does not preclude the use of sterling. Since 1999, more and more reproductions are including both 925 and sterling. A piece with both marks meets the requirements of both the EC and America, two huge markets.

English hallmarks

A typical English hallmark ca. 1890-1999, generally has four symbols and may have five. These symbols may be placed in any order. They include:

1) Symbol for the town in which the silver content was certified, called an assay or town mark.

2) Symbol for the year of manufacture, called the date letter.

3) Symbol representing the silversmith or factory which made the object, called maker's mark or sponsor's mark.

4) Symbol for the standard mark guaranteeing the silver content. The English silver standard is also 925/1000. It has been represented by the lion passant (looking ahead) since 1875.

5) Optional profile of the current king or queen.

To stay competitive with the EC nations, England has recently made several important changes to its hallmarking laws. The most significant change has been dropping the mandatory use of the passant lion as a standard mark. Beginning in 1999, England agreed the millesimal expression of the standard mark, 925, would be accepted. Mandatory use of the date letter was also dropped in 1999. Date letters are now optional in British hallmarks.

England has also agreed to accept standard marks on silver imported into England from any nation that signs a 1976 treaty, or convention, guaranteeing strict testing of silver content. These so-called convention hallmarks consist of a registered maker's mark and either two or three other marks: a control mark, a standard mark and, if the piece was made in England, an assay mark.

The control symbol used in convention hallmarks since 1976 is always a scale. The millesimal, or numeric expression of the standard, 925, must appear in the middle of the scale. Although the standard is expressed in the control mark, a separate stand-alone standard mark is still required. The separate standard mark may appear as 925 only or 925 enclosed in a simple shape such as an oval, square or circle.

If a piece was made in a foreign country for import into

Mid-19th century to ca. mid-1970s

| Maker's mark | Assay or town mark | Standard mark (silver) | Date letter |

Typical pre-1975 British hallmark. From left: maker's mark =symbol of silversmith or company; assay mark=symbol of the city in which silver content was tested, leopard head shown is London; standard mark=lion passant (looking ahead, to viewers left) certified that silver content was 925/1000. A fifth mark, the profile of the ruling king or queen, not shown here, is optional.

1976–present, export or sale in England

| Maker's mark | Control mark | Standard mark | Assay or town mark |

A typical hallmark on silver made in England for either export or sale in England. The control mark, a set of scales, was adopted in 1976. The scales mark certifies the acceptance of a 1976 treaty in which nations agreed to recognize each others hallmarks. Pieces with this mark can be exported from England to any country which has signed the same treaty. The standard mark can now be expressed numerically, or millesimally, as 925. The lion passant is no longer required but may be used in addition to the numeric mark. Pieces for sale in England, as well as for export, must also have an English assay mark.

1999–present, made/sold in England only

| Maker's mark | Assay or town mark | Standard mark |

Beginning in 1999, neither date marks nor the lion passant were required on silver made and sold in England. Date marks are now optional; the standard mark was replaced by 925. Pieces for export must include the 1976 convention hallmark, a scale.

Silver and Silverplate

International convention hallmarks, since 1976

| Control mark | Standard mark | | Maker's mark | Control mark | Standard mark |

Two typical so-called convention hallmarks. Characterized by the scale control mark and millesimal standard mark expressed as 925. Mark on right has optional maker's mark. Any piece of silver with the scale control mark and 925 standard mark may be freely traded among all nations agreeing to or signing the 1976 convention, or treaty, regulating hallmarks. These marks are accepted in Europe, England and the United States.

England, it would include a maker's mark, control mark and standard mark. But if a piece was made in England for sale at home, it would require a fourth mark, a British assay mark.

These changes may sound confusing at first, but are of great benefit. It gives the collector and dealer who understands them specific permanent marks to establish firm dates of production.

Fake and forged marks

Although you can catch many reproductions simply by understanding laws that regulate marks, that assumes the marks themselves are honestly applied. Forgeries attempting to copy genuinely old marks are somewhat harder to detect. The difficulty in detecting such marks is generally related to the skill and knowledge of the forger.

The silver marks most widely forged are generally those which have the potential for the greatest increase in value. The Tiffany and Unger Bros. forgeries shown in this chapter are typical of two frequently targeted high-value names.

The best way to catch these carefully prepared forgeries is a side-by-side comparison. Compare the mark of a suspected piece to genuine marks in reference books or known originals in your own collection. For example, marks on Tiffany silver generally include both an order number and a pattern number. Many forged Tiffany silver marks do not include either an order number nor a pattern number (see examples later in this chapter).

You can also catch many forgeries by knowing how original marks were applied. Almost all marks on almost all antique and collectible silver and silverplate were applied with stamps. Unique, individual or custom marks–such as serial numbers, order numbers, artists marks, hallmarks, etc.–were generally made with hand-struck punches, each punch bearing a single letter, numeral or symbol.

Larger marks with several lines or large symbols could be struck by hand or a machine press. Most marks on silverplate, regardless of the size of the mark, were mostly struck by machine presses because the base metal was heavier and stronger than solid silver. Complex marks, like the Tiffany example previously discussed, may include both standard company marks found on all pieces, as well as unique marks for individual pieces such as an order number, pattern number, date letter and others.

If this sounds like a lot of work, it was. It also involved a great deal of highly specialized equipment. Fortunately, most forgers don't have the time or the money to duplicate original vintage marks so they take shortcuts.

The most common shortcut is to cast, or mold, a mark rather than stamp marks. If you make a single mold with an old appearing mark, every piece made in the mold will carry that mark. That process saves both the time it would take to stamp a mark on each new piece, as well as the expense of the stamps and other necessary equipment.

Some of the most common cast forgeries of old marks in the market today are found on figural napkin rings. Cast, or molded, marks almost always lack the detail found in stamped marks. Cast marks tend to be shallow with ragged or blurred edges and uneven in depth of impression. Original stamped marks are just the opposite: clean sharp edges with an almost perfectly uniform depth of impression. Several examples of new molded marks are shown next to the original stamped marks later in this chapter.

At the current time, faked cast marks are more commonly found on new silverplate than silver. Pieces of silver with fake marks tend to be found on simply shaped objects easily cast as a single piece. These include thimbles, brooches, tussie-mussies, charms, needle cases and other similar pieces.

The biggest danger in detecting new molded marks is to stop your examination after you have matched a suspected mark to marks in a reference book. Molds made from originals produce copies with original appearing marks. You must examine how

Five common warning signs of new, fake or forged marks

1

Any mark that is badly blurred or badly worn is suspicious. Many of these marks appear in areas where no logical normal wear would occur. Blurring and smudging is often used to make forged marks illegible, especially maker's marks and date marks. Yes, natural wear is expected on older pieces, but wear should be normal and logical. New hallmarks above from a new match safe.

2

Any standard mark that includes 925 is suspicious. All 925 marks, whether standing alone or combined with other symbols as the above example, are very nearly a guarantee of a reproduction. The 925 standard mark was very rarely used in vintage American silver. It was not widely used until the European Community (EC) adopted it in the mid-1970s.

3

lead pencil

Any mark that is exceptionally small is suspicious. The 925 standard mark above is smaller than the diameter of the lead in the wooden pencil shown for comparison. Any mark under one-sixteenth of an inch is suspect.

marks are made, as well as how the mark reads. This is especially important if your original mark is a line drawing and not a photograph.

English hallmarks-special considerations

Faked English hallmarks are being found on more and more pieces of new sterling silver. First, the international and convention marks–the scales and .925–are removed. Then the forged

4

Any mark applied by soldering a tab, disc or other shape should be thoroughly examined. The oval tab marked sterling shown here is soldered to a new rattle. Some authentic Victorian-era silverplated pieces do bear applied discs (above right) with the manufacturer's name. However, even those discs should be examined very carefully. Many genuinely old discs with marks have been removed from inexpensive common pieces and applied to more expensive, but originally unmarked pieces.

5

New–cast   Old–stamped

Any mark formed by casting, not stamping, is suspicious. Virtually without exception, authentic marks on vintage silver and silverplate were stamped, not cast. Reproductions, particularly new silverplate, are generally cast in molds. Since new molds are usually made by copying originals, marks on originals are usually transferred to the new molds. Cast marks are almost always blurred with impressions of uneven depth. Stamped marks are generally much cleaner and sharper than cast marks.

hallmarks are applied. Many buyers see what appear to be English hallmarks and assume the piece is quite old, or at the very least, made before 1975 when the international convention marks were introduced.

You can often detect many forgeries of English hallmarks simply by knowing how and where authentic marks were placed. On objects formed of more than one piece, for example, hallmarks were required to be placed on the main or primary section and the secondary section. This includes removable lids on covered

Silver and Silverplate

A full set of English hallmarks appears on the inner lip of this authentic silver match safe: maker's mark, city mark, standard mark, year date. An abbreviated set of marks—the standard mark and date letter—appear on the hinged lid directly above the main mark.

dishes, coffee and tea pots, as well as hinged sections on match safes, tankards and similar shapes.

On authentic English silver, you should typically find a full set of marks on the primary section consisting of maker's mark, standard mark, assay mark and year date. The secondary section, such as a lid, typically should include two marks, the standard mark and the year date. Location of the secondary marks varies. Sometimes the secondary mark is close to the primary mark; in others, it may take some looking.

Beginning in early 2001, there were many forged English hallmarks being applied to new silver including match safes and shapes of other Victorian novelties. None of those forgeries had secondary marks. Although the presence of a secondary mark does not prove a piece is a forgery, a secondary mark is generally a positive sign of a correctly applied English hallmark. Any piece of English silver made in more than one piece generally should be marked twice: one full set of hallmarks in the primary section, and a second set of hallmarks, usually a year date and standard mark, on the secondary section.

Another example of a full set of English hallmarks on the primary section of an authentic piece of vintage English silver.

Matching secondary marks to the primary marks shown in photo above. Secondary marks are inside the lid.

English lion vs. Netherlands lion

The English hallmark for 925 silver content is a lion with upraised paw looking ahead, to the viewers' left (passant). Required until 1975.

 **English**

The Netherlands lion silver standard hallmark is similar to the English lion. The Dutch lion faces to viewers' right and includes the numeral 2. The Dutch lion certifies .833 silver content. Dutch lion hallmark used ca. 1814-1953.

 Netherlands

General guidelines

As a practical matter, it is almost impossible to remember all the names, forms and variations of silver marks. General line dealers and casual collectors can probably avoid most mass produced silver fakes in today's market by following the guidelines outlined on the previous pages.

On this and following pages are examples of marks frequently seen on new silver. Most of these marks contain obvious features such as size, lack of detail, a convention mark, or the 925 standard mark, that will help you identify pieces as new.

Keep in mind genuine marks on 19th and early 20th century silver and silverplate vary considerably in appearance and new marks frequently change in response to the market.

Silver and Silverplate

African Silver

A mark found on English silverplate, ca.1850-1900.

Alaska Metal

Trade name for silverplated flatware sold by Sears Roebuck & Co., from ca. 1908 forward.

Albu Silver

A British manufacturer of plated-brass novelties, from ca. 1880s. This company was still in business in the mid-1990s.

Aluminum Silver

Trade name of Daniel and Arter, Birmingham, England, for a non-silver alloy.

AN makers mark

This new silver dog whistle has the two separate hallmarks shown below, marks A and B. Mark A left to right: maker's mark, AN; assay mark (leopard head=London); 925 standard mark, lion passant; voluntary date letter, U. But you don't need to look up the date letter to know the piece is modern. Mark B is a typical convention hallmark used only since 1976. Mark B, left to right: scale control mark; 925 standard mark. Both marks are very small–both marks fit on the jump ring on dog's nose; only about one-thirtieth of an inch high.

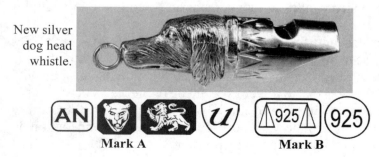

New silver dog head whistle.

Mark A   Mark B

Sterling and Silverplate

Typical Atocha silver "coin" with confusing marks. These include 1) "ATOCHA"; 2) date "1622"; 3) sterling quality or standard mark, 925. Atocha does not appear on any Spanish coins. The date 1622 is when the Atocha sank; Atocha pieces were made after 1990.

1994 advertisement for Atocha silver coin jewelry.

Atocha

The Atocha was a Spanish treasure ship recovered in the 1980s. Most of the treasure was in the form of silver bars. Rather than sell the bars as bullion, or scrap, the silver was cast into the shapes of 17th century Spanish coins and made into jewelry such as earrings, bangle bracelets and other shapes.

Each of the "coins" in the jewelry is marked with the date, "1622," "Atocha" and 925. As the years have passed, a number of Atocha pieces have drifted into the collectibles market. People see the date and assume the pieces are old. Other pieces are deliberately altered by removing the findings–like earposts, hanging loops, etc.,–and intentionally representing the piece as a coin

The date of 1622 is when the ship sank, not when the "coin" was made. Any piece marked Atocha is not earlier than ca. 1990. The 925 mark never appeared on vintage Spanish coins. A 925 was struck on the Atocha pieces because they met the American and European silver standard for silver content, 925/1000. Most Atocha pieces were sold with elaborate "certificates," with the true facts buried in very small print.

Silver and Silverplate

Bengal Silver

Trade name of Daniel and Arter, Birmingham, England, for a non-silver alloy.

Brazil Silver

Another name for nickel silver, most commonly called German Silver, a non-silver alloy made of copper, zinc and nickel with a silvery-white appearance. Also appears under the name Solid Brazil Silver.

Brazilian Silver

Trade name of Daniel and Arter, Birmingham, England, for a non-silver alloy.

Bristol Silver

Trade name for a silver look-alike made by Bristol Mfg. Co., Attleboro, MA., ca. 1895-1915.

CME maker's mark

CME maker is not known. The scale, or control mark, indicates the country of origin has signed the 1976 convention. Any item with the scale mark cannot date earlier than the mid- to late-1970s. Full mark is shown below.

CME

The reproduction, shown here, is sterling silver with the CME hallmark. The original was nickel-plated brass. No original has ever been documented in sterling silver.

Coin silver

Coin silver refers to objects made of silver obtained from melting coins. Silver from coins, having been alloyed with hardening agents to withstand circulation, has a silver content of 900/1000. This compares with the higher sterling standard, 925/1000, which was softer.

American silversmiths were forced to use melted coins because of a shortage of silver bullion in the early 19th century. The silver shortage was caused by a lack of ore from any American mines and the refusal of foreign sources to sell bullion to American silversmiths to limit competition.

The use of melted coins was at its height from about 1850 to the late 1860s. By the late 1860s, newly discovered silver mines in Nevada and with the U.S. government requiring certain foreign tariffs and duties be paid in coin or bullion, the shortage of silver ended. With more silver available, American silversmiths began upgrading their silver content to the higher 925/1000 standard and marking their wares sterling to reflect the higher silver content.

Coin silver was never a governmental standard or legally required mark; it is only a generic name used by collectors. It is virtually impossible you would ever find "coin silver" as a mark

Fake silver pins all marked "coin silver" on back. Left to right: "Western Atlantic RR, Confederate States of America;" "KKK" figural with date of 1867; "Andersonville Guard 2, Confederate States of America."

Photos courtesy P. Bertram, The Confederate Medals, Buttons & Ribbons Newsletter *and N. Rossbacher,* North South Trader's Civil War Magazine.

 Fake "coin silver" mark on present-day fakes. No authentic pieces made ca. 1850-1860s are marked "coin silver."

Silver and Silverplate

The most common authentic mark on genuine American coin silver made 1850-1860 is simply the word "coin," usually with a maker or merchant name. Examples shown above with coin and maker initials, left; coin and hallmark of Gorham silver, right.

Two more authentic marks of vintage coin silvers. "Standard" with maker initials above, left. "Pure silver coin" with maker and city name in mark above, right.

on vintage flatware, holloware or jewelry made, ca. 1850-late 1860s. The only time period in which "coin silver" was regularly applied to jewelry and other small items, is ca.1920-30s on pieces made in small home shops, particularly by Southwestern native Americans and Mexicans.

The most common genuine marks on authentic American coin silver are the words "coin," and "standard;" other authentic marks include "pure silver coin," and, occasionally, the word "dollar."

The mark "coin silver" has been appearing on recent fakes including the three pieces shown on the previous page, purporting to have been made during the American Civil War and shortly afterwards. No old counterparts to these fakes are known.

Continental Nickel Silver

Same as nickel silver, most commonly called German Silver, a non-silver alloy made of copper, zinc and nickel with a silvery-white appearance.

DAB

Reproduction figural silver match safe, right, with traditional English hallmark below. Reading mark left to right: maker's mark, DAB maker's mark; standard mark, lion passant; assay mark, London; date stamp, 1993. DAB is the mark of contemporary English silversmith David Bowles. Any piece with this maker's mark cannot be earlier than the mid-1970s.

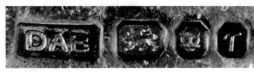

D & A, Daniel and Arter

Birmingham, England. This hallmark-style mark may appear with a variety of confusing trade names that contain the word "silver." Some of the names are Aluminum Silver, Indian Silver and Japanese Silver. At most, pieces with these names are silverplated. No silver was used in the alloys from which these pieces were made.

D & A

Empire Art Silver

A trade name of E & J Bass, New York, NY, ca. 1890-1930. The company made both sterling and silverplate, but this mark appears mostly on silverplated base metals.

Silver and Silverplate

England Silver

Found on pieces made of nickel silver, commonly called German Silver, a non-silver alloy.

EPBM

Electro Plate on Britannia Metal, see EPNS below.

EPNS

EPNS is a mark for Electro Plate on Nickel Silver. Silverplating on nickel silver was another way to imitate pure silver flatware and holloware. Manufacturers of these wares came up with a variety of marks to identify these pieces. Many of the marks copy the general appearance of hallmarks used on sterling silver. Two typical examples are shown here.

EPNS-Electro Plate on Nickel Silver appearing in a hallmark-style mark.

EPBM-Electro Plate on Britannia Metal. Very fanciful hallmark-style mark of J. Dixon & Sons, Sheffield, England.

G Silver–German Silver

The most common name for a non-silver alloy made of copper, zinc and nickel with a silvery-white appearance. Also called nickel silver. Although vintage items may be marked German Silver, not all items marked German Silver are necessarily old. There are many variations of names used for nickel silver.

Some of the more unusual include Brazil Silver, Panama Silver and Yukon Silver.

G (in diamond)

First reported at end of 2001. No old counterpart of the G hallmark is known. This match safe was one of many new sterling silver items with the G in diamond mark being sold in English markets in late 2001. Exact source of manufacture unknown.

GJ (in diamond)

First reported in the spring of 2001. No old counterpart of the GJ mark is known. The mark was first found on a group of new silver match safes with sports themes. Several of the pieces were close copies of known original shapes. The golfer match safe shown here imitates an original by Gorham. Exact source unknown.

Silver and Silverplate

Japanese Silver

Trade name of Daniel and Arter, Birmingham, England, for a non-silver alloy.

JM, James Mackie

Silversmith James Mackie has been making reproductions of figural silverplated napkin rings since 1992. Many of the rings are direct copies from Victorian-era original. Mackie's reproductions include moving wheels, silver wire reins on animals and other details usually found only on Victorian originals.

New silverplated napkin ring by James Mackie, above. One version of Mackie's hallmark, below.

There are at least two marks. One is a simple JM inside a box. The other is somewhat more elaborate with the letters separated by a crown. Many of Mackie's hallmarks are extremely small, some measuring about half the diameter of the lead in a wood pencil.

Laxey Silver

Trade name of Daniel and Arter, Birmingham, England for a non-silver alloy.

Meriden Silver

This new Meriden mark is found on a figural silverplated napkin ring. A mold taken from an original ring captured the original mark in the new mold. Every new piece now produced in the mold has what appears to be an original mark which included the model number, 199. Original marks are stamped. Letters and numbers in original stamped marks have sharp edges and the depth of impression is uniform. Molded marks are almost always blurred, rough and the depth of impression varies.

New molded mark.   Old die-stamped mark.

Mexican silver
A non-assayed mark, no guarantee of silver content.

Nearsilver
Trade name by unknown maker for nickel silver, a non-silver alloy.

Nevada Silver
Trade name of Daniel and Arter, Birmingham, England, for a non-silver alloy.

Oregon Silver
A mark found on English silverplate, ca. 1880.

Pairpoint
See main entry in the Art Glass chapter which includes marks on Pairpoint silverplate.

PAJ
PAJ is the mark of an unidentified maker/importer. Pieces with this mark were widely sold throughout the U.S. ca. late

261

Silver and Silverplate

1980s-early 1990s. Most pieces with the PAJ mark are reproductions of antique shapes and designs like the 1½-inch locket shown. No similar mark is known to exist pre-1980s. The presence of the 925 mark is a clue to this piece's recent manufacture.

Panama Silver

Found on flatware made of nickel silver, most commonly called German Silver, a non-silver alloy made of copper, zinc and nickel with a silvery-white appearance.

Pearl Silver

Found on flatware made of nickel silver, most commonly called German Silver, a non-silver alloy made of copper, zinc and nickel with a silvery-white appearance.

REO

REO is a silver wholesaler located in the U.S. Products made with its design in various countries are usually marked REO plus the copyright symbol, © and the word sterling. About 50-60 percent of the product line is based on antique shapes such as sewing novelties, stamp boxes, pill boxes, chatelaines and other shapes like the figural suitcase stamp box shown below. All very good quality. No vintage silver is marked REO.

Roger Smith

"Roger Smith" is a forged mark. It attempts to copy 19th century original marks of the famous American family of silversmiths with the last name of Rogers, ending in the letter "s." Two of the many vintage marks including the word Rogers are shown here for comparison.

Old | **New**

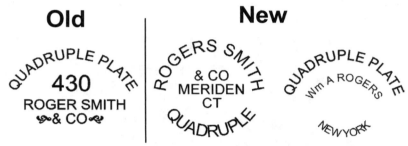

Forged Roger Smith mark. | Two vintage marks with the name Rogers, ending with the letter "s."

Siberian Silver

A mark found on English silverplated copper, late 19th century.

Silvanir–see Silverine.

Silverine

Silvanir and Silverine are two separate trade names for look-alike silver items produced by Nov-E-Line Mfg., New York. Estimated production ca. 1890-1910.

Silveroin

Trade name for a non-silver alloy made by Bristol Mfg. Co. Attleboro, MA, ca. 1895-1915.

Silver and Silverplate

Simpson Hall Miller

The new example shown was found on a silverplated napkin ring. This new mark was cast, or molded. Most new cast marks are produced from molds taken from original pieces. Any piece made in the new molds will reproduce the old marks. All authentic marks are die-stamped like the original mark shown below. True stamped marks have sharp-edged details and an even, uniform depth of impression.

New molded mark.   Old die-stamped mark.

Solid Brazil Silver

Found on flatware made of nickel silver, most commonly called German Silver, a non-silver alloy made of copper, zinc and nickel with a silvery-white appearance. Also found as Brazil Silver.

Solid Yukon Silver Warranted

Trade name on silverplated wares made by Raymond Mfg. Co., Muncie, IN, no production after 1920.

Sterline

Trade name for a silver look-alike made by James E. Blake Co., Attleboro, MA, ca. 1902. Name appears in at least two different versions as shown here.

Sterlon

Trade name of Milton J. Schreiber, New York, NY. First used 1949. Found on silver alloys and plated wares.

STERLON

Tiffany & Co

Tiffany is a frequent target for forgeries because of its high value. Generally, most original Tiffany silver marks include both a pattern and order number. In the original mark shown below, the pattern number appears on the left of the word Makers; the order number appears to the right (see white arrows). Note that the individually stamped order and pattern numbers are not perfectly aligned, a typical sign of custom stamping.

Original Tiffany silver is of the highest quality. If you discover poorly soldered joints, seams or other flaws on a piece that is marked Tiffany, you should immediately become suspicious.

Generally, most original Tiffany silver marks include both a pattern and order number. In the original mark, right, the pattern number appears on the left of the word Makers; the order number appears to the right (white arrows).

This fake was first reported in Silver Magazine *by Janet Zapata. Reprinted by permission of* Silver Magazine, *Inc. and Janet Zapata.*

Tiffany Studio New York

The fake Indian Police silverplate badge on the next page is marked "Tiffany Studio New York" on the back. A close-up view of the mark is shown below the badge. No old counterparts like this cheap badge were ever made by Tiffany. The same piece is also available in brass (bronze). Wholesale price $5. In the market at least since the early 1990s.

Silver and Silverplate

**TIFFANY STUDIO
NEW YORK**

In the faked mark, "Studio" is singular, not plural. The original mark is plural, "Studios." But no such item as this badge was ever made by Tiffany. This badge is a complete fantasy item; no old counterpart was ever produced.

Unger Bros.

New silver brooch, below right, appears with forged Unger Bros. mark shown below left. An original Unger Bros. mark is also shown below for comparison. The new Unger mark has a large dot in the bottom of the letter U. The fake is made from two pieces of silver. First, the lady's head was die-stamped, then a sheet of silver was soldered on the back.

This fake was first reported in Silver Magazine *by Janet Zapata. Reprinted by permission of Silver Magazine, Inc. and Janet Zapata.*

Larry Stanley Photo

New   Old

The new mark on left appears on the new brooch above. Note the large dot in the bottom of the letter U. The original mark shown at right for comparison. This is one of the few authentic marks in which 925 is used. Note, however, that 925 does not appear alone but with the company mark of Unger Bros.

Sterling and Silverplate

Here's another new piece copied from an Unger original, a new silver match safe. The new mark on the match safe is somewhat similar to the intertwined UB found on some original Unger pieces. The new match safe and mark are on the left; the originals are on the right.

New  **Old**

Utah Metal
Found on flatware made of nickel silver, most commonly called German Silver, a non-silver alloy made of copper, zinc and nickel with a silvery-white appearance.

Wolf Silver
Found on flatware made of nickel silver, most commonly called German Silver, a non-silver alloy made of copper, zinc and nickel with a silvery-white appearance.

Yukon Silver
Found on flatware made of nickel silver, most commonly called German Silver, a non-silver alloy made of copper, zinc and nickel with a silvery-white appearance.

Foreign Words and Phrases

With very little effort, foreign words and phrases can offer powerful clues of an item's country of origin, probable dates of manufacture and whether it might be a reproduction. Most of this information can be drawn from translations of words such as *patent*, *copyright*, *corporation* and others used in regulating businesses in almost all countries.

These terms have always been and continue to be fairly tightly controlled by governments around the world. Their presence–stamped, molded, printed or painted–on an object tends to reduce the possibility of it being a fake or forgery. On the other hand, place-names of regions or countries which no longer exist–such as Suhl, Nippon, Limoges, Staffordshire, etc.,–can legally be used on new pieces. Knowing what words are proper for which countries can help you detect fake marks and provide identification of originals.

Another benefit of understanding commonly used foreign words is to gauge a seller's honesty and knowledge. Simple words for patents and copyrights are sometimes represented as the proper names of manufacturers and artists. The most common example is the word *Musterschutz* found on German steins. This term only means "copyrighted design" as most collectors and dealers in steins know. However, many general line dealers and auctioneers confuse the term with a maker's or artist's mark and use the word as an adjective such as, "..a fine *Musterschutz* stein."

That is the equivalent of saying "...a fine *copyrighted design* stein." Musterschutz doesn't imply either age or quality; it is simply an ordinary, everyday term used by government clerks and lawyers to regulate business and commerce.

Another cause for concern is the widespread change taking place in Europe after the fall of Communism and the division of the Soviet Union. Free of central domination from Russia, many East European nations either have changed or are in the process of changing their name. For example, the names *Czechoslovakia*, *Czech Republic* and *Republic of Czechoslovakia* are all very similar but represent three distinct time periods over a span of 80 years.

This chapter includes a list of foreign words typically found in marks with an emphasis on French and German terms but also covering Spanish and Italian words plus other selections. In addition to legal terms, translations are also given for words that commonly appear in inscriptions such as Happy Birthday, Happy Anniversary, etc.; words that appear in labels such as rice, coffee, wine, etc.; and familial terms like brother, sister, father and so on.

Keep in mind that some terms and words do not have an exact American English counterpart. In those cases, the closest general meaning is given.

An auction advertisement listed "a fine bronze button signed Brevette." Brevette is the French equivalent of Patented. Brevette, of course, appears on many items including this bronze button.

Is this the original box for the toy inside? Blechspielwaren is German for "metal toy." If the toy in the box isn't metal and isn't from a German maker, there's a problem.

The difference between
Depose and Deponiert

Both the French *depose* and the German *deponiert* are abbreviated as DEP. The three letters appear on many items of all price ranges and quality from inexpensive celluloid novelties to mega-buck bisque dolls.

Some reference books, particularly toy and doll books, incorrectly imply that the DEP abbreviation is associated with particular firms or makers or limited to the particular subject under discussion (bisque dolls, penny toys, etc). By itself, the DEP abbreviation can mean *either* France or Germany.

Generally, the appearance of depose, deponiert and DEP on consumer products other than printed media, declined after WW I and for most purposes ceased altogether during WW II. Since mid-20th century, most copyrighted and protected designs are marked with the © copyright symbol or ® registered symbol. Although some United States designs, particularly character toys, have used © since ca.1920s, most foreign-made items with © indicate they have been made since ca. 1950.

French
depose = registered

German
deponiert = registered

Examples of abbreviations for both Depose (French) and Deponiert (German). Other numbers or words may often appear with the DEP abbreviations and can sometimes help determine the country of origin. The example on the far left includes "GES" which is an abreviation for the German word "Geschutz." This means Germany is the source of this DEP mark. You'll find similar words listed and explained in the following pages of this chapter.

Foreign Words and Phrases

Alphabetized words in bold followed by English translation then native language in italics. *Ger*=Germany, *Span*=Spanish and so on. The abbreviation c/c is used to represent the English words "company" or "corporation."

Abteilung department *Ger*
AE Anonimos Eteria c/c *Greece*
aG auf Gegenseitigkeit c/c *Ger*
AG Aktiengesellschaft c/c *Austria, Ger, Switz*
A/L Andelslag c/c *Norway*
Allee avenue *Ger*
Allemagne Germany *Fr*
allumette match *Fr*
A.m.b.a. c/c *Denmark*
Angleterre England *Fr*
anniversaire birthday *Fr*
AO Anonim Ortakigi c/c *Turkey*
A&P Assn et Participation c/c *Belgium*
ApS Ampartsselskab c/c *Denmark*
argent silver *Fr*
argento silver/silver ware-argenteria *Italy*
artificiel artificial *Fr*
artificiale artificial *Italy*
A/S Aksjeselskap Aktieselskab c/c *Norway/Denmark*
A.S. Anonim Sirketi c/c *Turkey*
atelier studio *Fr*
Ausgabe/Ausg. edition *Ger*
BA c/c *Netherlands*
bébé doll in the image of a baby *Fr*
bébé nus naked (undressed) doll *Fr*
biere beer *Fr*
Bier beer *Ger*
Bierglasuntersatze beer coaster *Ger*
biru beer *Japan*
birra *Italy*
Blechspielwaren metal/tin toys *Ger*
Blumentopf flowerpot/vase *Ger*
bonbonniere sweetmeat/candy box *Fr*

Foreign Words and Phrases

brevete patented *Fr*
brevetto patent *Italy*
Bruder brother *Ger*
Butterdose butter dish *Ger*
B.V. c/c *Netherlands*
C. de R.L. c/c *Spain*
café coffee *Fr*
cafetiere coffepot *Fr*
caffe coffee *Italy*
cannette tankard/stein *Fr*
cann coffee cup *Fr*
carton-pate cardboard/pasteboard *Fr*
Cia/Companhia/Compania c/c *Brazil, Portugal, Spain*
Cie./Compagnie Company *Fr, Belgium, Luxemberg*
contraffazione fake (painting) *Italy*
contrafacone forgery *Fr*
corbeille gifts to bride from bridegroom *Fr*
cristallerie glass factory *Fr*
cuir leather *Fr*
cuir moule shaped leather *Fr*
cuivre copper *Fr*
cuivre battu wrought copper *Fr*
cuivre jaune brass *Fr*
CV Commanditaire Vennootschap c/c *Nethrlnd*
Czech Republic1990 forward, formerly Czechoslovakia
Czechoslovakia, Czecho-Slovakia first used 1918 to 1939
décore a la main hand decorated *Fr*
décore par decorated by *Fr*
deponiert registered (deponier) *Ger*
dépose registered *Fr;* marque déposée-registered trademark
deutsch German (Deutscheland, Germany) *Ger*
diritto d'autore copyright *Italy*
D.P.A. patent applied for *Ger*
D.R.G.M. registered/patented, pre-1918 *Ger*
D.R.P. German patent *Ger*
Edms Bpk Eiendoms Beperk   c/c *S Africa*
eG eingetragene Genossenschaft c/c *Ger*

eGmbH c/c *Ger*
eingetragen registered *Ger*
émail enamel (paint) *Fr*
enfant child *Fr*
Englisch English *Ger*
E.P.E. c/c *Greece*
Eirinn Ireland *Irish* (Deanta in Eirinn=made in Ireland)
étain tin/pewter (d'etain) *Fr*
Etats Unis United States *Fr*
Ets. Etablissement c/c -*Belgium, Fr*
e.V. eingetragener Verein c/c *Ger*
Falschung fake (falschen) *Ger*
falsificare forgery or fake *Italy*
faux imitation/fake (fausse) *Fr*
flammefest flame/heat resistant *Ger*
fabrikmarke factory mark *Ger*
falsificacion forgery *Span*
fille girl/daughter/unmarried young woman *Fr*
fils son *Fr*
Firenze Florence *Italy*
fabrique par manufactured by *Fr*
foyer hearth or home *Fr*
Frankreich France *Ger*
Franzosisch French *Ger*
fraude fake (falso) *Span*
frére brother (fréres, brothers) *Fr*
garniture de toilette decorations/accessories for
     dressing table or boudoir *Fr*
GbR Gesellschaft burgerlichen Rechts c/c *Ger*
Geburtstag birthday *Ger*
Gegr. established/founded *Ger*
Gebruder brothers (abbreviated, Geb.) *Ger*
Gegen Nachbildung Geschutzt copyright/registered *Ger*
German silver (see Silver chapter in this book)
Gesellschaft c/c *Ger*
Gesetzlich Geschutzt Ges/gesch copyright/registered *Ger*
Geshundheit health/sanitary *Ger*

Foreign Words and Phrases

GmbH/GMBH c/c *Ger Austria, Switz*
Glashuttenwerke/Glassmanufaktur glass factory *Ger*
Glockewagen bell cart (toy) *Ger*
grés stoneware *Fr*
HB Handelsbolag c/c *Sweden*
HF Hlutafelag *c/c Iceland*
Heim home *Ger*
Heirat marriage *Ger*
hochfeine high quality/fine quality *Ger*
Holz wood *Ger*
Honigdose honey jar *Ger*
Humpen tankard/stein *Ger*
imitazione imitate *Italy*
imitar imitate *Span*
keramische ceramic *Ger*
jahrestag anniversary *Ger*
joaillier jeweler *Fr*
jouet toy *Fr*
Junge young boy *Ger*
Juwelen jewelery *Ger*
Juwelier jeweler *Ger*
Kaffee coffee *Ger*
kaffeekanne coffeepot *Ger*
KB Kommanditbolag c/c *Sweden*
Kind child *Ger*
KK Kabushiki Kaisha c/c *Jap*
Knabe boy *Ger*
kunstlich artificial *Ger*
Kupfer copper *Ger*
lampadaire floor lamp *Fr*
lamp de bureau desk lamp *Fr*
letters patent *British*
Liqueursatz liquor set *Ger*
Ltee. Limitee c/c *Canada*
Maatschappij c/c *Netherlands*
Madchen girl *Ger*
mari husband *Fr*

mariage marriage *Fr*
marchio di fabbrica trademark *Italy*
marke trademark/factory mark *Ger*
Marqué de fabrique trademark *Fr*
mécanique mechanical *Fr*
mére mother *Fr*
mikrowellen microwave safe, since ca.1970's *Ger*
Munchen Munich *Ger*
Musterschutz copyright/registered *Ger*
Mutter mother *Ger*
Nachahmung imitation *Ger*
Natale-Christmas albero di Natale Christmas tree *Italy*
Noel Christmas *Fr*
Nr number *Ger*
or gold (d'or = golden) *Fr*
orfévre goldsmith or silversmith *Fr*
oro gold *Italy*
Papierstoff papíer mâche *Ger*
parfum perfume *Fr*
parfumeur mfr/seller of perfume *Fr*
patente patent *Span*
patine patina (on bronze) *Fr*
Pfeffer pepper *Ger*
pére father *Fr*
Pére Noel Santa Claus *Fr*
planfonnier celing light *Fr*
plateelbakkery pottery studio *Dutch*
poivre pepper *Fr*
porzellanfabrik (porzellanwerke) porcelain factory *Ger*
porcelaine fabrique porcelain factory *Fr*
prost! to your health/cheers *Ger*
Pte Private c/c S*ingapore*
poupée doll *Fr*
P.V.B.A c/c *Belgium*
reg Gen mbH   c/c *Austria*
Reis rice *Ger*
remedar imitate, mimic *Span*

Foreign Words and Phrases

Republic of Czechoslovkia 1948-ca.1990 (also see Czech Republic)
riz rice *Fr*
RP Reichspatent, a goverment. patent *Ger*
rouages clockwork *Fr*
rue street *Fr*
SA de CV c/c *Mexico*
SA Societa Anonima c/c *Italy*
Salz salt *Ger*
Salzglasiert saltglaze pottery *Ger*
SAS Societa in Accomandita Semplice c/c *Italy*
Saugling baby *Ger*
sautoir long narrow necklace *Fr*
schale bowl/platter *Ger*
Schlottern baby rattle *Ger*
Schutzmarke trademark *Ger*
Schweizer Switzerland (Swiss) *Ger*
Schwester sister *Ger*
SdnBhd Sendirian Berhad c/c *Malaysia*
seau (seaux) ice pail, used as flower vase *Fr*
sel salt *Fr*
Senfkanne mustard pot *Ger*
Silber silver *Ger*
S/L Salgslag c/c *Norway*
S.N.C. Societe Non-Collective c/c *Fr*
sociedad corporation *Span*
Sohn son *Ger*
souer sister *Fr*
S.p.A. Societa per Azioni c/c *Italy*
Spielwaren toys/playthings *Ger*
Spielzeug toy *Ger*
SSK Sherkate Sahami Khass c/c *Iran*
Ste societe c/c *Fr*
steingurfabrik stoneware factory *Ger*
Steinzeug stoneware *Ger*
Strasse street *Ger*
sucre sugar *Fr*

SV Samenwerkende Vennootschap *Belgium*
Streicholz match *Ger*
tabakstopf tobacco jar *Ger*
Tchecoslovaquie Czechoslovakia *Fr*
taillé cut (e.g. cut glass) *Fr*
te tea (teiera-teapot) *Italy*
tazza de te tea cup *Italy*
Tee tea (teekanne-teapot) *Ger*
thé tea (théiere-teapot) *Fr*
Tochter daughter *Ger*
Tschechoslowake (Tscheche) Czechoslovakia *Ger*
Uhrwerk clockwork (windup) *Ger*
vajilla de cristal glassware *Span*
Vater father *Ger*
VEB People Owned Factory, 1948-1990 *E Ger*
Venezia Venice *Italy*
verrerie glass works/shop *Fr*
verrier glass worker/glass maker *Fr*
vesta match (vesta box-matchbox) *British*
vetrame glassware *Italy*
vetro glass *Italy*
vin wine *Fr*
VVB Assn. Peoples Own Entprs., 1945-91 *E Ger*
Waschbar washable *Ger*
Weihnachten Christmas *Ger*
Weihnachtsmann Santa Claus *Ger*
Wein Vienna, *Austria*
Wein wine *Ger*
Werkstatte workshop/studio *Ger*
West Germany used from 1948-1991
YK Yugen Kaisha c/c. *Jap*
Zettel label *Ger*
Zinn tin/pewter *Ger*
zucchero sugar *Italy*
Zucker sugar *Ger*

Trademarks, Logos and Brand Names

Many collectors specialize in the products, premiums or advertising material of specific companies. Some of the more popular are Winchester, Keen Kutter, Griswold and similar manufacturers.

Many otherwise ordinary products—such as pipe wrenches, pocket mirrors and watch fobs—can literally be worth their weight in gold (and sometimes more) when bearing a collector's prized trademark. The bad folks know this and a small cottage industry has grown up around adding highly collectible trademarks and brand names to genuinely old, but originally unmarked, objects by other low-value manufacturers.

Right now, fake paper labels of vintage trademarks are a particular problem. Low-cost image manipulation software makes it easy to scan and alter originals found in reference books. Local or regional names and addresses are easily added to original images. The new images are then printed out on high-quality inkjet or laser printers and sold as advertisements, premiums or applied as labels to unmarked objects.

Many of these fakes can be caught with common sense and logic. Old scratches run over and through old marks. Old scratches are stopped or covered by new labels or die-stamped marks. Close up photos of examples appear throughout this chapter.

This new Keen Kutter trademark was applied on top of an old gouge (arrow). If the trademark had been on the piece since it was manufactured, the gouge would go through the mark, the mark would not go over the gouge.

Courtesy Rilla Simmons

Arcade

Arcade was the first manufacturer of coffee grinders to include hoppers made of glass so the amount of coffee beans was visible. The original Arcade #4 grinder, shown here, was sold from about 1900 until the Depression of the 1930s.

The glass receiver jar is the hardest original part to find and demand has always been great by owners trying to assemble a complete grinder. Demand has apparently been strong enough to inspire someone to make reproduction jars.

Complete Arcade model #4 wall mounted coffee grinder. Clear glass hopper above holds beans; glass receiving jar below (arrow) catches the ground coffee.

Bottom of new receiver jar does not include "Freeport ILL" embossed below the 4.

Bottom of original receiver jar includes "Freeport ILL" embossed below the number 4.

Trademarks, Logos and Brand Names

Cheinco

Many reproductions from the 1970s and 1980s of early advertising trays and signs were produced by Cheinco Housewares. Its log cabin-style mark appears below. This mark is about one-half inch tall. There is no old counterpart to this mark.

This mark should not be confused with J. Chein & Co. marks found on pre-WW II toys and banks.

The Cheinco Housewares mark, above, is permanently printed on the reproduction metal serving tray, right, featuring Clysmic Water.

Desperate Enterprises

This company specializes in antique reproductions of all kinds. It sells a wide range of new metal signs, new pieces based on early advertising and copies of country store objects. Many, but not all pieces are marked. Any object with its mark is new, made since the 1980s at the oldest.

New

The piece at left is a typical new product by Desperate Enterprises. A full-color Uncle Remus paper label is wrapped around a metal can; there is a coin slot in the top for use as a bank. The paper label, as shown above, is marked Desperate Enterprises Inc. in very small letters.

Walt Disney

Almost every officially licensed Disney product–vintage or modern–has a copyright notice, either the word "copyright" or the copyright symbol, ©. Licensed products made before 1939 are marked Walt Disney Enterprises. "Enterprises" is sometimes abbreviated Ent. After 1939, products are marked "Walt Disney Productions" or "WDP."

The Disney mark may or may not include the companies or manufacturers granted the license. Typical company names that appear in vintage marks are Sun Rubber, Lionel, Fisher Price, Marx, Linemar and other similar names.

Most classic Disney collectibles, ca. 1930s-1960s, were made in the USA, Japan and Germany, not China. The great majority of reproductions made since the mid-1980s have been made in China. Any Disney products marked "China" cannot possibly be much more than 10-15 years old at most.

The mark on most licensed products being made today is simply the copyright symbol, ©, and the word Disney. The country of origin may or may not appear with © Disney.

Of course, Disney marks are found on licensed products only. Unlicensed, or bootlegged, products will generally not have any marks or might even have deliberately forged old-appearing marks.

Pre-1939	1939–present
Copyright	Copyright
Walt Disney Enterprises	Walt Disney Productions
© Walt Disney Ent	© Walt Disney Prod

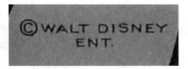

In current use

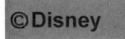

Most new products today are marked with only the copyright symbol and Disney.

© Disney
YOUNG EPOCH
MADE IN CHINA

Vintage pre-1970 Disney collectibles were never made in China.

281

Trademarks, Logos and Brand Names

Door knobs

Genuinely old door knobs in porcelain and glass are being etched with trademarks and logos of highly collectible companies. The etching is about one-sixteenth of an inch deep below the surrounding surface. After etching, the artwork and lettering are inked in matching colors: Coca-Cola is red, Ford is blue, etc. No old doorknobs are known that resemble these new products.

Some of the trademarks being used include Coca-Cola, Ford, Chevrolet, Pepsi-Cola, Harley-Davidson, John Deere and Dr. Pepper. Others are sure to exist. This technology can apply similar etchings to virtually any ceramic or glass surface. The old metal hardware with the etched knobs are left dirty, rusty, and tarnished which adds to the appearance of age.

Chevrolet in blue and Pepsi-Cola in red etched into genuinely old white porcelain knobs. Both knobs 2¼-inch diameter.

"Drink Coca-Cola" etched into both clear glass knobs and colored red.

Ford oval logo etched into both knobs and colored blue.

282

Fisher Price

Some of the earliest and most highly sought after Fisher-Price wood pull toys are being reproduced. Two of the first have been the #795 Mickey Mouse Drummer originally issued in 1937 and the #185 Donald Duck Xylophone originally issued in 1938.

The most reliable way to separate old from new is by examining the Fisher Price trademark. The originals also have the early Disney marks (also see Disney listing in this same chapter).

Trademarks on Fisher-Price reproductions are exactly the same as on originals. Original model numbers are also used. However, because the reproductions are made in China, they do not include "Made in USA" or American patent information.

Original Fisher-Price trademark with original model number includes "Made in USA" and American patent information (black arrow). Reproductions do not include USA anywhere on the toy.

G Whiz–Braniaks, Inc

A mark that appears on reproductions of classic 1950 metal lunch boxes. Some of the new boxes include The Lone Ranger, Space Cadet and Howdy Doody. Most of these pieces are also marked Made in China. Vintage collectible lunch boxes were made in the USA.

Trademarks, Logos and Brand Names

Griswold Manufacturing Co.

Griswold was one of the main cast iron foundries of the U.S. The company specialized in products for the home, especially items for the kitchen. Various pieces have been reproduced with markings used by the original company.

Three typical new cast iron pieces are shown here. They include a #0 toy skillet, an 8½-inch Stick pan and the #50 Heart-Star pan. All of these reproductions are marked like originals.

Generally, new pieces have a coarse, pebbly texture. New marks typically have poorly formed letters of uneven depth and irregular shape. If rust is present, rust on new cast iron is usually a reddish-brown. The carbon content of vintage cast iron is different from modern pieces. Rust on vintage pieces is typical brown or brown-black.

Bottom of reproduction Griswold toy skillet, size 0, model 562. Same markings as on the original.

Bottom side of fake Griswold cast iron Corn or Wheat Stick baking pan, 8½- by 4¼-inches. Original made 1932-1950s is the same size with the same markings.

New #50 Heart-Star pan. Originals sell for $1,500-$2,000. Reproductions wholesale for about $15.

Keen Kutter

The Keen Kutter brand name was developed by the Simmons Hardware Company of St. Louis, Missouri. The brand dates back to 1870 when it was first used on tools and cutlery. As original Keen Kutter items have become collectible, the Keen Kutter trademark has been included on many reproductions and forged on genuinely old but unmarked items from other manufacturers.

The official trademark is a wedge with a horizontal bar through the middle and Keen Kutter in slanted lettering. With few exceptions, this wedge-shaped trademark appears on every authentic item. If an authentic item does not have the wedge mark, it is most commonly due to the shape of the object. Long, thin shapes like wrench handles and ruler blades, for example, may have only the Keen Kutter lettering.

It is very important to note what name, if any, appears at the top of the wedge. This name changed over the years and can be used for approximate dating. The different names that appear in authentic marks and the approximate years the changes were made are shown on the opposite page.

Keep in mind that dates of trademarks are approximate. Items already made before name changes continued to be sold by new owners. In an interview with Russell Meeks, current president of Val-Test, Meeks said some Keen Kutter items marked Shapleigh's existed in such large quantities that they continued to be sold into 1965 and beyond.

Authentic Keen Kutter trademarks should be well formed, well proportioned and legible no matter what the size or how it is applied. A half-inch die-stamped mark in a knife blade, an 8" acid etched mark on a glass display case, or a printed paper sign should all

Courtesy Rilla Simmons

Fake Keen Kutter trademark applied to old stoneware jug. The logo has been sandblasted or otherwise etched which leaves the letters raised above the surrounding background. The background is painted red.

285

Ca. 1870-1940
Simmons
Hardware

1940-ca. 1960s
Shapleigh's Hardware

1965-1985
Val-Test Dist. Inc

Since 1985
licensed to various mfrs.

From 1870 to 1940, E.C. Simmons appears at the top of the wedge-shaped trademark. After Shapleigh Hardware bought Simmons in 1940, Shapleigh's name replaced Simmons. Val-Test Distributors, Inc. placed the traditional trademark on a large letter K, 1965-1985. Since 1985, Val-Test has licensed the wedge-shaped trademark to a number of present-day manufacturers. No company names currently appear in the wedge-shaped trademark of officially licensed products.

be equally legible.

Virtually all pre-1960 trademarks should include either "E.C. Simmons" or "Shapleigh's" at the top of the wedge. The words "St. Louis, U.S.A." or "Cutlery and Tools" frequently, but not always, also appear inside the pointed area of the wedge. Their use, however, varied considerably in pre-1960 originals and are not as an important indicator of age as either E.C. Simmons or Shapleigh's.

A faked Keen Kutter paper dial created on a home computer was put on this low-value unmarked alarm clock from the 1930s.

The "scratches" on the faked dial are printed in black ink. In other words, the forgers began by scanning in an old scratched clock face and adding the Keen Kutter trademarks.

Detail of faked paper label on scale. How could the paint *under* the label be scraped and chipped and the label still remain without a scratch? If a new label was added at the time the scale was manufactured, the label would logically be subjected to the same wear as the scale.

An ordinary ca. 1930s kitchen scale with faked paper labels on both sides. A somewhat similar genuine scale does exist that is marked Simmons Hardware, but no scale like this was ever originally made with the Keen Kutter trademark.

287

Trademarks, Logos and Brand Names

Courtesy Rilla Simmons

Two new wooden yard sticks. Top: "Use Shapleigh's Keen Tools Cutlery" with wedge-shaped trademark. Bottom: "Use Shapleigh's Diamond Edge Tools Cutlery" with Diamond Edge trademark. Diamond Edge was a trade name of Shapleigh's. Both yard sticks mass-produced by advertising speciality manufacturer.

Fake mark on cast iron boot jack. Note the Made in China tag which is on the piece as it arrives from the reproduction wholesaler. All authentic Keen Kutter trademarks, whether antique or modern, will appear with a wedge.

L–in gear

The letter L in a gear symbol is printed on new tinplate toys made since the early 1990s. The majority of toys with this mark are reproductions or look-alikes of 1950s and pre-WW II toys.

The same L mark is also stamped on metal keys included with new windups. The L keys will fit many vintage toys and may show up as a replacement key.

LA Stamp

All trade tokens and advertising pieces marked "LA STAMP" are fakes. Many pieces marked LA STAMP also have late 19th and early 20th century dates and use trademarks and logos of highly collectible companies such as Coca-Cola, various brands of liquor, railroads and firearms manufacturers. LA STAMP items have been in the market since the early 1980s. Although most fakes occur as tokens, the mark can also appear on other advertising-related products.

The LA Stamp mark is fairly inconspicuous. Any piece with this mark is a fake.

Fake Kentucky Derby token; reverse marked LA Stamp.

LA Stamp research and photos courtesy David Schenkman. David writes a regular column for the TAMS Journal, *the official publication of the Token and Medal Society*

Lutted's Cough Drops

James Lutted of Buffalo, New York, was a leading candy maker and wholesaler of retail display cases and candy jars. The "J.L." cough drop was one of the biggest sellers and was displayed in a log cabin jar (right) embossed with the company name.

Original Lutted Cough Drop covered cabin-shaped jar.

The log cabin pattern was made by Central Glass Company of Wheeling, West Virginia, which introduced it around 1875. The original pattern was called simply Pattern #78.

Trademarks, Logos and Brand Names

Top view looking down into new Lutted base, left. Bottom of new base has molded texture of wood grain, but no lettering. Old base has "JAS. LUTTED BUFFALO NY U.S.A." in bottom. There is no molded wood grain in bottom.

New

Old

The new lid is marked, "Lutted's S.P. Cough Drops" only.

Original lids are marked "Lutted's S.P. Cough Drops" too, but also have the additional words, "Genuine Has J.L. Stamped on Each Piece."

Reproductions of the Lutted log cabin jar have been made since about 1991. New and old can be separated by the markings on the roof and on the base as shown in the photos.

Marlboro Pewter

The mark Marlboro Pewter, Canada, is found on new pickle castor frames manufactured in Canada. The frames have been made there since early 2000.

Frames of almost exactly the same style were sold by the LG Wright Glass Co. ca. 1960-1990 with new glass inserts. Wright frames are not marked.

Old Sleepy Eye

Old Sleepy Eye collectibles are premiums, advertising items and promotional pieces from the Sleepy Eye Milling Company of Sleepy Eye, Minnesota. The town's name and the company's distinctive trademark were based on a Sioux Indian Chief, Old Sleepy Eye. Founded in 1883, the company continued in operation till 1921.

Reproductions of Old Sleepy Eye collectibles have been in the market since the late 1960s. Some, like the many paper reproductions, are fairly simple. Others, like pieces of pressed glass, are quite ambitious and require special molds.

The most notorious items in pressed glass are a paperweight, jar and tumbler. All three shapes were made from a new

The mold used to make the reproduction Old Sleepy Eye glass jar, tumbler and paperweight.

mold constructed ca. 1974. New shapes include a 5¼-inch jar, a 2¾-inch paperweight and a 4-inch tall tumbler. All items are in clear glass. Each piece has a molded portrait of Chief Sleepy Eye and the words Old Sleepy Eye. Production was carried out by St. Clair Glass of Elmwood, Indiana. The majority of pieces are crude

New "advertising mirror" made with an inexpensive button-making machine. The full color paper image is protected by a plastic covering, then crimped down over a round mirror.

291

Trademarks, Logos and Brand Names

New pressed glass Old Sleepy Eye fantasy pieces made during the 1970s. From lower left, 2¾-inch paperweight, 4-inch tall tumbler and 5¼-inch jar. All items are in clear glass. Most pieces are very crude with obvious bubbles and streaks in the glass.

clear glass with many bubbles.

There are no old counterparts to these three pieces nor are they authorized reproductions from any celebration, collectors club or centennial.

Probably the most common Old Sleepy Eye reproductions are made of paper. Paper requires no mold and is relatively cheap to produce. The majority of paper fakes today are being made on home computers with digital imaging software (see index under Old Sleepy Eye for related products).

There are several generations of reproduction barrel labels. The latest from the year 2000, left, is made into a 16-inch cardboard sign, printed both sides with two holes for hanging. The first reproductions, right, appeared during the Sleepy Eye, MN, centennial celebration in 1972. Printed one side on paper.

Shaker Seeds

Most collectors associate the Shakers with products such as furniture, quilts, household gadgets, farming tools and implements. Many may not realize the Shakers were responsible for many firsts such as condensed milk, flat brooms and offering seeds for sale in paper packages.

The wooden boxes Shakers crafted to display their seeds in 19th and early 20th century country stores are very collectible. And while their furniture was rarely, if ever, marked, Shaker seed boxes and seed packages were almost always marked or labeled.

New display boxes with Shaker Seed paper labels have been available for several years. Labels on most new boxes have been reproduced from originals.

New labels virtually always fluoresce under long wave black light. Most new labels are seamed; originals are one piece.

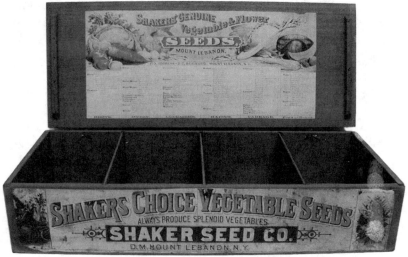

New 22-inch wide seed box marked "Shakers Choice Vegetable Seeds, Shaker Seed Co., D.M. Lebanon." Label on inside lists seeds available.

Many new Shaker seed labels are made from more than one piece of paper. Original labels were almost always made of one piece of paper.

Trademarks, Logos and Brand Names

Winchester

Winchester Repeating Arms Co. made more than just fire-arms. At the end of WW I, the company began making a variety of new consumer products to maintain wartime production levels. New products included a variety of tools, sporting goods, and other items unrelated to the original firearms business.

All those products, like the company's famous rifles, were marked Winchester. It has become very common for originally unmarked but genuinely old items by other companies to show up with faked and forged Winchester marks.

The great majority of all authentic Winchester products were marked with the company's distinctive trademark composed of jagged-edged letters.

WINCHESTER

The original Winchester trademark is formed of distinctive jagged-edged letters, the so-called "lightning letters" trademark.

Forged Winchester mark stamped on an originally unmarked wrench by another manufacturer.

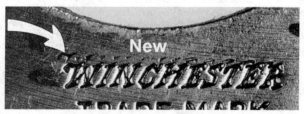

Detail view of forged mark from wrench above. The forged mark was applied by hand-striking a stamp. The stamp bounded leaving a double strike. Notice the shadow of the double strike above the word Winchester (arrow). Original marks were applied with a machine press and never show a double-strike.

Old

Original Winchester wrench with authentic die stamped lightning letter trademark. Authentic die-stamped marks are virtually never found with double-strikes. All letters are properly aligned and stamped to a uniformly even depth.

Most forgers use the same size mark regardless of the size of the piece to which the fake mark is applied. Original marks were a number of different sizes, proportional to the piece to which they were applied. The faked mark above is too small for this wrench.

Similar sized wrench showing an authentic mark, proportional to the surface to which it was applied. This original mark is about twice the size of the fake.

Old

Authentic Winchester pipe wrenches are marked twice on the front side–on the movable jaw, top arrow, and on the frame, bottom arrow.

Many new "marked" pipe wrenches are formed by taking an originally unmarked wrench and switching the jaw from an authentic marked wrench. That creates one wrench with an unmarked frame and a marked jaw, and another wrench with a marked frame and an unmarked jaw.

All wrenches courtesy Bailey Collection, ACRN photos.

The fantasy saddle watch fob, top, is marked with the forged Winchester trademark shown directly above. This piece comes from the wholesaler with the forged mark already applied.

Fantasy baseball glove and bats watch fob, top, comes from the wholesaler marked "Winchester Sporting Goods The Winchester Store" shown directly above.

Another new watch fob marked "Winchester." No original Winchester die-stamped mark appears in quotation marks.

Appendix

©–Copyright symbol which gives notice that a design or pattern is filed with the U.S. Copyright Office. Items of foreign manufacture may carry this mark to protect their designs shipped to and sold in America. Appears ca. 1910-1915 until present.

Dishwasher Safe– Dishwashers came into fairly widespread home use in the early 1960s. The higher water temperatures used in dishwashers can damage earlier glazes and decorations.

®–Registration symbol which gives notice a mark or design has been filed with U.S. Patent and Trademark Office. Used since ca. 1950 through the present.

™–A notice of trademark ownership which may be used with or without a formal filing with the U.S. Patent and Trademark Office.

Zip code– A system of sorting US mail by five-digit numeric codes attached to end of the last line in an address. Zip code was authorized in 1963 but not mandatory until 1967. Some large cities used three-digit local codes, but not zip codes, prior to the national zip code system launched in 1963.

PRC-China The PRC, or Peoples Republic of China, is mainland China, or Communist China. Communist China was established in 1949 when forces under Mao Tse Tung forced the Nationalist China leader, Chiang Kai-shek, to flee to Taiwan. China is a source of a huge volume in antique reproductions. Items from the PRC are most often marked Made in China and occasionally PRC.

ROC-Taiwan The ROC, is the Republic of China, also referred to as NRC, National Republic of China. The ROC was formed on the island of Taiwan, formerly Formosa, after the 1949 defeat of Nationalist China forces on the mainland. Taiwan built itself into a major manufacturing center during the 1950s and was a major source of antique reproductions in the 1970s-1980s.

West Germany-East Germany East and West Germany reunited as the single country Germany in 1992. Many reproductions formerly easily recognized by the mark West Germany, are now marked Germany only, similar to old pre-WWII marks.

Index

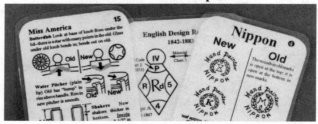